W9-BSX-233

the
marketing
performance
blueprint

the marketing performance blueprint

strategies and technologies
to build and measure
business success

paul roetzer

WILEY

For general information about our other products and services, please contact our
Customer Care Department within the United States at (800) 762-2974, outside the
United States at (317) 572-3993 or fax (317) 572-4002.

Wiley publishes in a variety of print and electronic formats and by print-on-demand.
Some material included with standard print versions of this book may not be
included in e-books or in print-on-demand. If this book refers to media such as a CD
or DVD that is not included in the version you purchased, you may download this
material at http://booksupport.wiley.com. For more information about Wiley
products, visit www.wiley.com.

Library of Congress Cataloging-in-Publication Data:

Roetzer, Paul, 1978–
    The marketing performance blueprint : strategies and technologies to build and
measure business success / Paul Roetzer.
        pages cm
    Includes bibliographical references and index.
    ISBN 978-1-118-88343-3 (Hardback); ISBN 978-1-118-88358-7 (ebk);
ISBN 978-1-118-88357-0 (ebk)
    1. Marketing–Management.   2. Strategic planning.   I. Title.
    HF5415.R5666 2014
    658.8'02–dc23

                                                                    2014022278

Printed in the United States of America

10 9 8 7 6 5 4 3 2 1

For Eila and Balen.

Contents

SECTION III MARKETING TECHNOLOGY

SECTION IV MARKETING STRATEGY

Foreword

When Brian Halligan and I started HubSpot in June 2006, we wanted to transform how organizations acquired customers. The Internet had altered how people accessed information, connected, shopped, and shared. As a result, marketing as we knew it was broken.

Traditional, outbound marketing methods, such as trade shows, advertising, and telemarketing, were becoming less and less effective. Consumers were choosing when and where to interact with brands, turning to search engines and social networks for resources, products, and services.

HubSpot became our chance to revolutionize the marketing industry and give businesses the tools needed to better reach and engage buyers online and on their terms.

It was around this time that I met Paul at the inaugural INBOUND conference in Boston. He was one of HubSpot's earliest adopters, and in 2008, his marketing agency, PR 20/20, became our first Agency Partner, helping to pioneer a program that now includes more than 1,500 agencies worldwide.

Paul and his team have worked with dozens of clients to build and execute performance-driven inbound marketing campaigns. We share a common belief that businesses need to outthink, rather than outspend, their competition. Playing by everybody else's rules is a surefire way to lose, whereas innovation—and thinking differently—is rewarded.

Consumers are more informed, in touch, and in charge than ever before. Outdated marketing methods interrupt and annoy, causing customers to move further away from brands.

Buyers crave personalized experiences, and brands need to up their game to connect with audiences in meaningful ways. They must transform marketing from something most people *hate* to something that they *love*. This requires a shift in marketing strategy.

Successful marketing programs focus on the people behind each transaction. They humanize marketing and reimagine the full customer experience, from first interaction to post-sale support. This is how you deliver memorable inbound experiences that turn followers into customers and customers into advocates. This is how you create marketing that people love.

But, there is no magic wand to transform obsolete marketing practices, and too many companies remain frozen in time. Marketing departments must evolve their mindsets and put the right technology and culture foundations in place.

Technology has dramatically changed how consumers live, connect, and shop, but it has also enabled marketers to execute more intelligent and targeted strategies. With technology in their toolbox, marketers can better meet consumer demands for excellence at every touchpoint, personalize interactions based on context, streamline campaign execution, and accurately measure performance.

It is for these reasons that companies like HubSpot exist—to help you market better and smarter, and to help you delight customers.

While technology makes lovable marketing a possibility, it is marketers who make it a reality. However, modern marketers are hard to come by—especially those with exceptional talent and the hunger to learn and achieve. To attract marketing stars, you must first become the keeper of culture. Define your organization's set of shared beliefs, values, and practices, and use that as the jumping-off point. Culture is to recruiting as product is to marketing—the better the culture, the easier it is to attract and retain exceptional talent.

As HubSpot has grown through the years, to more than 700 employees today, I have spent significant time thinking about culture. So much so that I have joked with my colleagues that the "T" in my CTO title may actually stand more for "talent" than "technology." I have learned that knowing what your company believes and what makes it tick are paramount to attracting and retaining the right people.

And, a talented team, when paired with the right marketing technology and an evolved marketing strategy, completes the marketing-performance trifecta.

However, transformation is difficult. *The Marketing Performance Blueprint* is your guide to help accelerate success through marketing talent, technology, and strategy. Use it to build a performance-driven business and to create marketing that people love.

DHARMESH SHAH (@DHARMESH)
Cofounder and CTO, HubSpot
Coauthor, *Inbound Marketing*

Acknowledgments

The Marketing Performance Blueprint would not have happened without the incredible PR 20/20 team—Sam Brenner (@sambrenner2020), Dia Dalsky (@DiaDalsky), Allie Gottlieb (@alliegott), Mike Kaput (@MikeKaput), Tracy Lewis (@Tracy_J_Lewis), Angela Masciarelli (@Ang_Masciarelli), Jessica Miller (@jessica_joellen), Rachel Miller (@RachelAMiller), Keith Moehring (@keithmoehring), Taylor Radey (@TaylorLauren), and Sandie Young (@SandieMYoung).

Each one of them played a part in telling this story. They embody what it means to be a modern marketer. They challenge themselves to constantly learn and evolve, and they continually push the limits of what is possible when the art and science of marketing collide.

They inspire me every day to be a better professional, and a better person.

Introduction

■ UNDERPREPARED AND UNDERPERFORMING

The marketing industry is advancing at an unprecedented rate, creating seemingly insurmountable gaps in marketing talent, technology, and strategy.

At a time when marketers face increasing pressure to measure the return on investment (ROI) of their campaigns and connect every dollar spent to bottom-line results, they are largely underprepared and underperforming.

According to Adobe's 2013 report "Digital Distress: What Keeps Marketers Up at Night?," 68 percent of marketing professionals feel more pressure to show return on marketing spend, while only 40 percent think their company's marketing is effective. A mere nine percent strongly agree with the statement, "I know our digital marketing is working."[1]

But with obstacles come opportunities.

Marketing technology has changed the game. Organizations of all sizes have access to the tools and knowledge needed to grow more efficiently and intelligently, to outthink, rather than outspend, the competition.

The marketers who will redefine the industry in the coming months and years and be in high demand take a technical, scientific approach.

Marketing is now, as it has always been, an art form. But the next generation of marketers understands it can be so much more. These innovators are rewriting what is possible when the art and science of marketing collide.

■ BUILD A PERFORMANCE-DRIVEN ORGANIZATION

The Marketing Performance Blueprint presents the processes, technologies, and strategies to fill marketing gaps and build performance-driven organizations. It is a guide for marketers, executives, and entrepreneurs to advance their businesses, exceed ROI expectations, and outperform the competition.

Do not waste another minute or dollar with traditional thinking and conventional solutions. Soon, every company, including your competitors, will have the tools, talent, and processes to excel. But it is still early. Your organization has the opportunity now to differentiate and drive growth.

As you read, consider the following questions:

➤ Does your organization have the right marketing talent, technologies, and strategies to achieve its performance goals?

➤ Are your expectations for growth aligned with your organization's potential?

➤ Are there weaknesses in your business and marketing cores?

➤ Are you maximizing the return on your marketing investments?

➤ Do you have the right performance-driven agency partners who are immersed in marketing technology, continually infuse ideas to propel growth, and add critical expertise and skills to your marketing team?

➤ Are your resources and campaigns aligned with priority marketing goals?

➤ What are the opportunities for underdogs and innovators that lack the resources of their larger competitors?

➤ What can large enterprises do to stay on top as smaller competitors develop more modern marketing teams, more quickly adapt to marketing technology advancements, and build more intelligent and efficient marketing strategies?

■ ACCELERATE SUCCESS

This is a book about what is possible. It is about unlocking your potential as a marketer and accelerating success for your organization.

The marketing talent, technology, and strategy gaps are very real, and they are impacting your business' performance. Now is the time to take control.

Key findings and insights from dozens of industry reports, articles, books, and interviews are woven into *The Marketing Performance Blueprint*, along with analysis of in-depth marketing assessments from hundreds of marketers, executives, and entrepreneurs.

I draw on my personal experiences consulting for hundreds of organizations, from startups to Fortune 500 companies, and mix in lessons learned as a marketing agency owner. My goal is to give you the resources and tools to advance your marketing career and help move your organization's marketing forward.

Watch for the [+] symbol as you read. This indicates a template spreadsheet is available to download from performance.PR2020.com as part of the Marketing Performance Pack we have created to complement the book. This free resource features a collection of templates, including a marketing team skills assessment, scorecard, campaign center, and project center.

➤ Website: performance.PR2020.com
➤ Twitter: @PaulRoetzer
➤ Book hashtag: #MKTBlueprint
➤ Email: booknotes@pr2020.com
➤ LinkedIn: www.linkedin.com/in/paulroetzer/

Let's begin the journey.

Section I: The Backstory

➤ Chapter 1—Mind the Gaps—lays the foundation, presenting insight into how gaps in marketing talent, technology, and strategy are leading to the most significant gap of all: the performance gap.

➤ Chapter 2—Commit to Digital Transformation—discusses the digital transformation imperative and considers ways to overcome obstacles faced by businesses of all sizes.

Section II: Marketing Talent

➤ Chapter 3—Build a Modern Marketing Team—explores the rise of hybrid marketers and the impending talent war for tech-savvy marketing professionals.

➤ Chapter 4—Construct an Internal Marketing Academy—dives into an analysis of how universities are struggling to keep pace and how some academic outliers and online institutes are filling the education void. It presents a process for using internal academies to build performance-based cultures and nurture modern marketing teams.

➤ Chapter 5—Propel Growth through Agency Partners—assesses the marketing agency ecosystem and shares systems for finding and managing marketing agency partners.

Section III: Marketing Technology

➤ Chapter 6—Create a Connected Customer Experience—focuses on processes and technologies, including marketing automation and intelligence engines, to personalize the customer journey.

➤ Chapter 7—Manage the Marketing Technology Matrix—starts with the software as a service (SaaS) revolution and walks through how to navigate the ever-changing landscape of marketing technology solutions.

Section IV: Marketing Strategy

➤ Chapter 8—Perform a Marketing Assessment—presents the knowledge and tools to conduct a complete review of your organization's marketing potential and performance.

➤ Chapter 9—Develop a Marketing Scorecard—demonstrates how to create a customized marketing performance measurement and reporting system for your organization.

➤ Chapter 10—Strategize a Marketing Game Plan—features a deep dive into the principles and processes of building more personalized and agile marketing strategies using the e3 (evaluate, establish, execute) framework.

Section

I

The Backstory

Chapter 1—Mind the Gaps—lays the foundation, presenting insight into how gaps in marketing talent, technology, and strategy are leading to the most significant gap of all: the performance gap.

Chapter 2—Commit to Digital Transformation—discusses the digital transformation imperative and considers ways to overcome obstacles faced by businesses of all sizes.

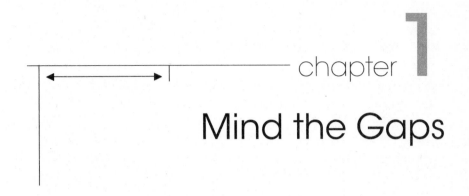

chapter 1

Mind the Gaps

We have entered the age of content, context, and the customer experience.

■ THE MARKETING TALENT GAP

Digital marketing has revolutionized the industry, and the job market. Corporate marketing departments, small businesses, and marketing agencies struggle to recruit and retain qualified professionals for career paths that did not exist three years ago, while academic institutions are faced with the need to adapt curriculums to the real-time nature of business.

The majority of professionals gain their digital marketing knowledge on the job rather than through full-time school programs. This lack of training and formal education is affecting marketers' confidence in their ability to execute critical digital marketing functions, including ecommerce, personalization and targeting, marketing measurement, social marketing, digital advertising, and content marketing.

In Search of the Unicorns

The job of every marketer, from the copywriter to the chief marketing officer (CMO), is to connect actions to

3

outcomes. However, according to the 2012 Marketing Skills Gap survey conducted by Focus (@Focus) and the Marketing Automation Institute, 75 percent of marketers say their lack of skills is impacting revenue in some way, and 74 percent say it is contributing to marketing and sales misalignment.[1]

In the 2013 report "B2B CMOs Must Evolve or Move On," Forrester (@forrester) and the Business Marketing Association (@BMANational) showed that 96 percent of marketing leaders believe the breadth of skills required to succeed in marketing has increased dramatically, and 44 percent say they cannot find the right combination of people and skills in the job market.[2]

Furthermore, Accenture (@accenture) found in its 2013 "Turbulence for the CMO" report that 39 percent of CMOs say they do not have the right people, tools, and resources to meet their marketing objectives.[3]

So, while marketers are charged with consistently producing meaningful results, including website visitors, subscribers, followers, leads, and sales, they often lack the fundamental skills, technologies, and strategies to unlock their company's potential.

Modern marketers must have a clear understanding of how their actions impact organizational goals. They are expected to continually expand their digital knowledge and capabilities, manage increasingly complex technology integrations, and devise strategies and campaigns that directly affect the bottom line.

Forward-thinking organizations seek hybrid professionals who are highly proficient writers, analytical, creative, and tech savvy, with strong competencies in business management, information technology (IT), and human behavior.

These next-generation professionals excel in emerging core-marketing disciplines such as analytics, automation, content marketing, email, mobile, and social networking. They envision on a strategic level, building fully integrated campaigns, and they have the capabilities to execute on the tactical level, performing activities that drive real business results.

But modern, hybrid marketers are a rare breed.

In his blog post "50% of All New Marketing Hires Will Be Technical," Scott Brinker (@chiefmartec), president and CTO of ion interactive (@ioninteractive), states, "There's a real scarcity of technical professionals, even more so for those with passion and aptitude for marketing."[4]

Brinker says, "There will be enormous competition for those unicorns, not just from other marketing departments, but from marketing software vendors, consulting firms, agencies, and a whole new bumper crop of start-ups, all of whom need this talent in pursuit of their missions."

Fill Marketing Talent Gaps

So, what can businesses do to fill marketing talent gaps and drive improved performance? Chapters 3 through 5 focus on marketing talent. We explore the evolution of the prototype marketer, the higher education story, internal academies, and the outsourcing option.

Here are examples of actions businesses can take to better attract, train, and retain modern marketers. We delve into each of these concepts in this book.

➤ Focus on culture and purpose as key factors to differentiate the company and attract top talent.

➤ Recruit professionals from nontraditional backgrounds, including economics, journalism, law, psychology, and statistics, and train them to be modern marketers. These individuals often possess critical core competencies, such as writing, strategic thinking, deductive reasoning, and understanding of human behavior, but are not marketers by trade.

➤ Capture applicants through website landing pages, which enable you to use analytics to monitor candidate engagement levels based on website interactions.

➤ Activate marketing automation tools to nurture candidates with prescheduled email workflows. For example, send applicants a series of emails with links to relevant company blog posts and content downloads. Then monitor to see which applicants take the recommended actions.

➤ Apply the same marketing technology used for lead scoring to rate and prioritize candidates based on brand engagement levels, such as content downloads, pageviews, email click-throughs, following social brand pages, and blog subscribes.

➤ Offer formal internal training programs to continually educate and evolve your marketers' capabilities. Teach your marketing team to take a scientific approach to marketing strategy, campaign management, and measurement.

➤ Maintain a performance-based culture in which marketers are assessed and compensated based on achieving marketing metrics. Challenge your team to always connect actions to outcomes.

➤ Use an internal social network to improve the marketing team's efficiency, productivity, and performance.

■ THE MARKETING TECHNOLOGY GAP

Marketers are being called upon to take leading roles in the selection, activation, and management of marketing technology solutions. Gartner Inc. (@Gartner_inc) forecasts that by 2017, the CMO will spend more on IT than the chief information officer (CIO) does.[5] This makes sense when you consider the array of marketing technologies required to build and measure business success:

➤ Analytics
➤ Call tracking

➤ Content management systems (CMS)
➤ Customer experience management (CEM)
➤ Customer relationship management (CRM)
➤ Ecommerce
➤ Email marketing
➤ Internal social networks
➤ Marketing automation
➤ Project management
➤ Search engine optimization (SEO) management
➤ Social media monitoring/management

According to a joint study by *MIT Sloan Management Review* (@mitsmr) and Capgemini Consulting (@CapgeminiConsul), "The world is going through a kind of digital transformation as everything—customers and equipment alike—becomes connected. The connected world creates a digital imperative for companies. They must succeed in creating transformation through technology, or they'll face destruction at the hands of their competitors that do."[6]

Marketers are becoming technologists, and the traditional-minded professionals and businesses that fail to adapt will become irrelevant.

But are marketers ready to assume the role?

Marketing software is a burgeoning space, being fueled by venture capital funding, mergers, acquisitions, and initial public offerings (IPOs). While the money accelerates innovation, it also creates a complex and fluid matrix of players and possibilities for marketers to navigate.

As the number of devices, screens, and channels expands, it becomes more difficult for marketers to create a connected customer experience. Marketers are often faced with the difficult decisions of best-in-breed versus all-in-one solutions, and legacy systems versus the latest and greatest. Siloed platforms and processes only widen the gap. Marketing technology systems must be integrated, with the ability to share and interpret data.

A strong marketing technology foundation is critical to driving performance. Fully integrated core-marketing technologies improve efficiencies, maximize productivity and return on investment (ROI), and create competitive advantages. Yet, many businesses lack, or are underutilizing, fundamental marketing technologies. For example, PR 20/20's "2014 Marketing Score Report" tells us:

➤ 53 percent of organizations do not have call tracking, which enables organizations to monitor and report offline conversions and assign full value attribution to the proper marketing channels.

➤ 41 percent of organizations do not have internal social networks, which strengthen internal communications, corporate cultures, employee relationships, and employee retention rates.

➤ 20 percent of organizations do not have marketing analytics, which means they have zero insight into online behavior, including visits, referral sources, page views, time on site, and conversions.[7]

Fill Marketing Technology Gaps

Chapters 6 and 7 take a comprehensive look at marketing technology. We cover processes to improve efficiency, marketing in a multiscreen world, the impact of marketing automation software, contextual content, leading solution providers, and integration best practices.

As you continue through the book, consider the value of these actions to create more agile and effective marketing campaigns.

➤ Appoint a chief marketing technologist or similar leader who drives and manages the convergence of marketing and technology within the organization.

➤ Assess your existing marketing technology infrastructure and identify steps to improve weaknesses.

➤ Build strong working relationships between IT and marketing teams to fully integrate critical technologies needed to run modern marketing campaigns.

➤ Develop processes to eliminate waste, such as underperforming programs and unproductive employee time.

➤ Invest time and money to move away from legacy marketing systems in favor of more agile software-as-a-service (SaaS) solutions.

➤ Use marketing software to create a connected experience throughout the customer journey.

■ THE MARKETING STRATEGY GAP

When Adobe asked more than 1,000 marketers, "What do you think will be most important to marketers in the next three years?" the most popular response out of 13 choices was social media marketing, at only 13 percent, with personalization and targeting second, at 12 percent. Content marketing, which is one of the hottest trends in marketing, came in 10th place at five percent.[8]

The lack of consensus could simply be attributed to variances in industry, budgets, company size, geographic region, or any number of factors, or it could be highlighting a growing strategy gap in which marketers lack the knowledge and capabilities needed to effectively prioritize activities and allocate resources.

B2C and B2B Consumers Take Control

We have entered the age of content, context, and the customer experience.

In what Google (@google) calls the "Zero Moment of Truth," consumers increasingly tap into the wealth of data and information available to them and research products in advance of purchases. Gone are the days when a marketing stimulus, such as an advertisement, direct mail piece, or cold call, leads directly to a sale. Google found that shoppers reference an average of 10.4 sources before making a purchasing decision.[9]

On the business-to-business (B2B) side, Forrester reports that buyers may be up to 90 percent of the way through their journey before contacting a vendor. "Marketing now owns a much bigger piece of the lead-to-revenue cycle. And B2B marketers must take responsibility for engaging with the customer through most of the buying cycle."[10]

Business-to-consumer (B2C) and B2B audiences crave knowledge, answers, and entertainment, while marketers strive to provide remarkable brand experiences that capture the hearts and minds of their prospects and customers.

Leading brands have become storytellers, seeking to engage and influence audiences in a real-time, multi-screen world, at all phases of the customer journey.

Marketers create videos, podcasts, blog posts, apps, webinars, newsletters, infographics, magazines, and events, all with the intention of connecting with audiences in more meaningful ways. They strive to create value, or, as author Jay Baer (@JayBaer) says in his *New York Times* bestselling book, *Youtility*, marketers aim to create content so useful, prospects and customers would want to pay for it.[11]

The new marketing imperative is to create more value, for more people, more often, so when it is time for consumers to choose a product, service, or company, they choose yours. When done well, brand content answers questions, inspires, and motivates audiences to take action, helping marketers to stand out from the competition. So, as marketers, all we have to do is become publishers, tell great stories, and give consumers the content they seek. Right?

Unfortunately, it is not that simple.

The marketing industry needs storytellers, but content creation and distribution is not enough. While content marketing gives us the ability to produce visitors, leads, and sales, marketers must go beyond storytelling to deliver personalized, highly relevant communications across all channels.

Next-generation marketers have a clear understanding of how their actions impact business goals. Closed-loop sales monitoring and analytics ensure marketers can tie activities to metrics that matter, accurately attribute customer conversions to the appropriate marketing channels, easily identify bottlenecks in marketing campaigns and sales processes, and continually improve over time.

Top marketers develop and activate assets at all phases of the marketing funnel. They build reach and brand at the top of the funnel, generate leads and convert sales in the middle, and retain customers and increase loyalty at the bottom.

Going Inbound

Inbound marketing is a term I use throughout the book. Made popular by HubSpot (@HubSpot), a Boston-based marketing software company with more than 10,000 customers worldwide, inbound marketing describes a more personalized and scientific approach to attracting, converting, and delighting consumers.

As consumers tune out traditional, interruption-based marketing methods and choose when and where to interact with brands, businesses must connect with consumers on their terms and create compelling customer experiences.

Inbound marketing takes a sophisticated, agile, and highly measurable approach to targeting consumers.

Strategies are fueled by analytics, automation, content, email, social media, and search. The core concept is to turn your website into a magnet that uses content marketing to draw in visitors, and then engage them through dynamic website copy, landing pages, calls to action, and automated and personalized emails.

Inbound marketing is designed to adapt to individuals at specific stages of the customer journey. It is meant to be more human, more personal, more intelligent, and more effective.

Going inbound is a critical step in building a performance-driven organization.

Fill Marketing Strategy Gaps

Chapters 8 through 10 present processes, tools, and resources to take a full-funnel approach to marketing strategy, conduct marketing assessments, build marketing scorecards, and devise performance-driven inbound marketing game plans.

Marketing high performers have better talent, more advanced technologies, and more intelligent and integrated strategies. Here are some examples of what leading organizations do to accelerate success:

➤ Adapt strategies and campaigns in real time based on analytics.

➤ Break down internal marketing silos and focus on a personalized and consistent customer experience across all channels.

➤ Drive business results through an integrated approach to analytics, automation, content marketing, digital advertising, email, mobile, search, social, PR, and web.

➤ Maintain advanced project/marketing management systems that connect actions to outcomes and enable dynamic campaign management and resource allocation.

➤ Run highly effective marketing automation campaigns.

➤ Take a full-funnel approach using a balanced campaign mix designed to build brand, generate leads, convert leads into sales, and increase customer loyalty.

➤ Use tracking and automation software to create personalized customer experiences across multiple screens and marketing channels.

HOW PROFESSIONALS RATE THEIR POTENTIAL AND PERFORMANCE

PR 20/20's "2014 Marketing Score Report" takes an inside look at how 318 marketers, executives, and entrepreneurs rate their organizations, using 132 factors across 10 sections.[12] The factor ratings (on a 0–10 scale) are combined with 27 profile fields, including annual revenue, revenue goals, marketing budget, employee size, industry, and sales cycle length, to provide strategic insights and help drive change and improved performance.

Key findings from the report demonstrate the challenges businesses face in achieving performance goals:

➤ The majority of organizations have aggressive growth goals and conservative marketing budgets, creating a potential misalignment of expectations.

➤ Organizations lack confidence in their internal marketing teams, which are particularly weak in key digital marketing skills.

(continued)

> ➤ Many organizations lack, or are underutilizing, fundamental marketing technologies, including call tracking, marketing automation, and marketing analytics.
>
> ➤ Key performance indicator (KPI) weaknesses at every stage of the marketing funnel affect the ability of organizations to achieve business goals.

■ THE MARKETING PERFORMANCE GAP

Talent Gap + Technology Gap + Strategy Gap = Performance Gap

Gaps in marketing talent, technology, and strategy are leading to the most significant gap of all—the performance gap. Marketers believe measurement is important, but most are struggling to do it well. Reaching and influencing customers, measuring campaign performance, and proving marketing ROI are among the greatest concerns to marketers.

The problem is, CMOs struggle to quantify ROI. According to Accenture's "Turbulence for the CMO" study, "nearly one in five score themselves as below average in multichannel attribution, correlating advertising to sales, and measuring media buying effectiveness."[13]

Fill the Marketing Performance Gap

So, if you feel overwhelmed, underprepared, understaffed, and under increasing pressure to perform despite the odds, you are not alone. Your peers and competitors face the same imposing marketing gaps.

Traditional talent, technologies, and strategies must evolve. This is your opportunity to reengineer your approach and reimagine what is possible for your business.

strive to provide remarkable brand experiences that capture the hearts and minds of their prospects and customers.

➤ The marketing industry needs storytellers, but content creation and distribution is not enough. While content marketing gives us the ability to produce visitors, leads, and sales, marketers must go beyond storytelling to deliver personalized, highly relevant communication across all channels.

➤ Inbound marketing is designed to adapt to individuals at specific stages of the customer journey. It is meant to be more human, more personal, more intelligent, and more effective.

➤ Gaps in marketing talent, technology, and strategy are leading to the most significant gap of all—the performance gap.

chapter 2

Commit to Digital Transformation

There has never been a better time to be a marketer.

■ ADOPTION AND ADAPTATION

The future of your business and your marketing career depend on your ability to meet increasing ROI demands and continually adapt to new marketing tools, philosophies, and channels. But the rate of change in the marketing industry is accelerating, and the challenges for marketers seem to be multiplying.

The marketing talent pool is underprepared, the marketing mix is evolving, and the matrix of technology providers is exploding. Customers are tuning out traditional marketing methods, while consuming information and making buying decisions on mobile phones, tablets, computers, smart televisions, and wearable devices. Marketers are drowning in data, dealing with the complexities of real-time marketing, and navigating brands through the openness and transparency inherent to social media.

Yet, there has never been a better time to be a marketer. Think about the possibilities.

➤ There is no more relying on meaningless metrics, such as impressions, ad equivalency, and PR value. Every action and interaction can be measured and connected to outcomes.

➤ Marketing software can eliminate wasted resources, improve productivity, and enhance performance.

➤ Websites can dynamically alter content at an individual visitor level based on historical behavior.

➤ Email communications can be automated and personalized.

➤ Leads can be scored and nurtured to assist sales and maximize conversion rates.

➤ Brands can gain unparalleled insight into consumer behavior, build publishing platforms to engage audiences, and adapt campaigns and budgets in real time based on performance.

In short, marketing can be more intelligent, measurable, and powerful. It can be an asset, not an expense. But change is not easy, and businesses of all sizes face an uphill battle.

■ OBSTACLES TO EVOLUTION

Marketing success requires a commitment to consistently create exceptional customer experiences, along with transparency, agility, and accountability at all levels. Unfortunately, many marketing leaders struggle to win and maintain internal support.

Let's take a look at some of the most common obstacles marketers face. All challenges can be overcome, but a starting point for many organizations is to understand the roadblocks that lie ahead and then develop strategies to address them.

Accountability

Marketing technology advances have made everything measurable. This can be intimidating for marketers who have never been held accountable for marketing metrics such as subscribers, leads, conversion rates, and sales.

According to the 2014 "CMO Survey," just 36 percent of CMOs have quantitatively proven the short-term impact of marketing spending, and for demonstrating long-term impact, that figure drops to 29 percent. So, the vast majority of CMOs use qualitative measures or have not been able to show an impact at all.[1]

Marketers must develop strong analytics knowledge and capabilities to continually prove the value of marketing to CEOs, CFOs, and the rest of the executive team.

Complacency

MIT Sloan Management Review and Capgemini Consulting teamed up in 2013 to survey 1,559 executives and managers on digital transformation, which they define as "the use of new digital technologies (social media, mobile, analytics, or embedded devices), to enable major business improvements (such as enhancing customer experience, streamlining operations or creating new business models)."

In the resulting report, "Embracing Digital Technology," researchers found that while 78 percent of respondents indicated that digital transformation will be critical to their organizations within the next two years, 63 percent felt the pace of change in their organizations was too slow. The most frequently cited obstacle was "lack of urgency."[2]

Ironically, success itself may be one of the largest culprits in creating complacent cultures. Too often, business leaders become comfortable with historical success and lack motivation to change their ways. They assume they can maintain market share, revenue growth, and profits by doing what has always been done.

But digital transformation has the power to upend industries and render market leaders obsolete. While the effects of staying the course may not be obvious in the short term, eventually complacent companies could pay the ultimate price. As the *MIT Sloan Management Review* and Capgemini Consulting study states in simple terms: "Adopt new technologies effectively or face competitive obsolescence."

Conservative Culture

There is an old axiom in the IT industry: "Nobody ever got fired for buying IBM." The idea is that IBM is a safe choice because it is a known entity. While newer and sometimes more innovative companies may come along with better features and products, IT departments have been conditioned to avoid risks and go with the status quo.

The same thinking can apply to marketing today: "Nobody ever got fired for placing an ad." Advertising, direct mail, trade shows, telemarketing, and other traditional activities are familiar. The risk is minimal, but so is the potential reward.

Differentiation and competitive advantage come from taking chances. Modern marketers are continually testing new technologies and strategies. While the probability of failure rises, so do the number of real-time learning opportunities. Analytics software gives marketers the insight to know what went wrong and the ability to make adjustments that improve performance.

As conservative organizations sit on the sidelines, modern marketers are capturing market share by activating marketing automation programs; building loyal subscribers, fans, and followers; developing mobile apps; engaging on social media; publishing blogs; retargeting website visitors with digital advertisements; and using branded content to educate leads and customers.

Businesses that are too slow to evolve and too afraid to take chances will lose in the long run. Conservative cultures can be corrected, but this change starts at the top. Leaders must provide the resources and runway to realize what is possible. Success does not happen overnight, so patience and persistence are essential.

History is full of industry leaders and business pioneers who have become irrelevant because they failed to innovate and evolve. Maybe it is the result of conservative cultures, poor leadership, a lack of will and vision, or the systematic inertia that builds from years of complacency. Or, possibly, they were just afraid. People fear the unknown. They resist taking the bold and decisive actions that are needed to survive because they do not want to fail. However, we learn from failure. It builds character, teaches us humility, shows us how to cope with adversity, and challenges us to continually test, revise, and improve.

—Paul Roetzer, *The Marketing Agency Blueprint*, p. 185[3]

Lack of Knowledge and Talent

As discussed in Chapter 1, the marketing talent gap has a direct effect on your business's ability to adopt new technologies and strategies and continually adapt to industry changes. To advance, you must attract a new breed of marketers (Chapter 3), build internal academies to evolve your existing marketing team (Chapter 4), and evaluate outsourcing to marketing agencies that bring complementary knowledge and skills to the mix (Chapter 5).

Power Struggles and Politics

Power struggles and politics are two unfortunate realities in business. Egos and self-interests can become challenges. If decision makers controlling the pace of change within the company lack confidence in their abilities to guide digital marketing transformation, then they may, consciously or subconsciously, hinder progress to preserve control and power.

Self-preservation is human nature, and it is a variable that must be considered. If you feel there are individuals or departments inhibiting progress, take steps to understand what elements of the process motivate and intimidate them. Use this knowledge to take a more strategic approach to change management that builds buy-in every step of the way.

Silos

Subscribers, fans, followers, leads, and customers choose when and where to interact with your brand. They do not differentiate between marketing departments and channels.

Think about all the possible consumer touchpoints. People may call, complete a web form, initiate an online chat, search a website for resources, download content, attend a webinar, subscribe to a blog, and/or connect on social networks. At each interaction, their needs and intentions are likely different. They are at a unique stage in their own personal journey with your brand, and yet, they expect the experience to be consistent.

Now picture how many different departments and individuals within your company affect the customer experience in the above scenarios.

With digital transformation and the shift to inbound marketing, the stakes are high. Marketing must break down its own silos (advertising, communications, content, digital, PR, SEO, social, web) and find innovative ways to collaborate with customer service, finance, human resources (HR), IT, operations, and sales to drive performance and create consistently remarkable customer experiences.

Legacy Systems and Technology Fatigue

As we will see in Chapter 7, the marketing technology matrix is vast and expanding at an exponential pace. According to Scott Brinker's 2014 "Marketing Technology Landscape Supergraphic," there are 947 different marketing software companies in 43 categories across six major classes.[4]

Keeping up with the latest and greatest tools is exhausting. While there are likely smarter ways to do pretty much every marketing function, from CRM to website content management, large enterprises have legacy solutions in place, and small and midsize businesses (SMBs) face budgetary and human resource challenges.

Change takes time, money, unwavering executive support, and an internal champion willing to wade through the politics and power struggles required to move the business forward.

High-performing companies are prepared for perpetual change. They put agile marketing teams and business processes in place that can scale and adapt as new technologies and opportunities emerge.

■ THE EXPOSED BRAND

We have entered a 24/7/365 bathing suit season in business. You and your company are always exposed, always vulnerable. Depending on your perspective, this can be intimidating or empowering.

Our lives and businesses have become reality shows— open to the world, sometimes by choice, other times by association. Customers are talking, competitors are watching, employees are networking, family and friends are sharing, and companies are scrambling to adapt and evolve.

We used to be able to avoid the spotlight, covering up our insecurities and masking our flaws. We could more easily control our brands and how we were perceived. But that was before the dawn of the digital age and the explosion of social networking.

At some point, we lost control, which is a scary thing for many marketers, executives, and entrepreneurs. We have been placed under the perpetual microscope of our social circles, in which the potential exists for unfiltered commentary and opinions about our every move, even if we choose not to participate.

Information is at our fingertips. What we discover online about people and businesses directly affects the decisions we make as professionals and consumers.

Job candidates, employees, business partners, academics, board members, executives, industry leaders, and media are all affected. No person or business, regardless of industry, is immune.

And yet, there are people who have never Googled themselves (or their brands) to see what others see, and there are companies that continue to ignore social media because they cannot calculate a direct ROI.

The Underdog Opportunity

What we all must accept is that everything has changed. That is, except for one immutable law: Perception is reality.

Whether you and your business are engaged in the online world or not, with every action you take and decision you make, you are either building or weakening your brand. This presents enormous challenges, but even more significant are the opportunities—awareness, engagement, goodwill, leads, loyalty, and love—for brands that have the confidence to "bare it all" and connect with audiences in more authentic and personal ways.

So, you have a choice.

Dive in: Be confident in yourself and take ownership of your brand. Accept that people are watching, talking, and judging, and embrace it to build your career and your business.

Cover up: Hide away with your fears, miss out on all the fun, and hope that you do not become irrelevant and obsolete.

This is no place for curmudgeons and lumbering organizations. This is the land of underdogs and innovators. Professionals and businesses that are nimble, dynamic, and transparent have the opportunity to disrupt markets, displace leaders, and redefine industries.

The next generation of leaders will be those who are ready to leave their comfort zones, let go of their fears and anxieties, take risks, and build remarkable corporate and personal brands.

The choice is yours.

CHAPTER HIGHLIGHTS

➤ The future of your business and your marketing career depend on your ability to meet increasing ROI demands and continually adapt to new marketing tools, philosophies, and channels.

➤ There has never been a better time to be a marketer.

➤ Inbound marketing success requires a commitment to consistently create exceptional customer experiences, along with transparency, agility, and accountability at all levels.

(continued)

➤ Marketers must develop strong analytics knowledge and capabilities in order to continually prove the value of marketing to CEOs, CFOs, and the rest of the executive team.

➤ Digital transformation has the power to upend industries and render market leaders obsolete. While the effects of staying the course may not be obvious in the short term, eventually, complacent companies could pay the ultimate price.

➤ Differentiation and competitive advantage come from taking chances. Modern marketers are continually testing new marketing technologies and strategies.

➤ Modern marketers are capturing market share by activating marketing automation programs; building loyal subscribers, fans, and followers; developing mobile apps; engaging on social media; publishing blogs; retargeting website visitors with digital advertisements; and using branded content to educate leads and customers.

➤ If decision makers controlling the pace of change within the company lack confidence in their ability to guide digital marketing transformation, then they may, consciously or subconsciously, hinder progress in order to preserve control and power.

➤ Marketing must break down its own silos (advertising, communications, content, digital, PR, SEO, social, web) and find innovative ways to collaborate with sales, finance, IT, customer service, and HR to drive performance and create consistently remarkable customer experiences.

➤ Change takes time, money, unwavering executive support, and an internal champion willing to wade through the politics and power struggles required to move the business forward.

➤ This is no place for curmudgeons and lumbering organizations. This is the land of underdogs and innovators. Professionals and businesses that are nimble, dynamic, and transparent have the opportunity to disrupt markets, displace leadership, and redefine industries.

Section

II

Marketing Talent

Chapter 3—Build a Modern Marketing Team—explores the rise of hybrid marketers and the impending talent war for tech-savvy marketing professionals.

Chapter 4—Construct an Internal Marketing Academy—dives into an analysis of how universities are struggling to keep pace and how some academic outliers and online institutes are filling the education void. It presents a process for using internal academies to build performance-based cultures and nurture modern marketing teams.

Chapter 5—Propel Growth through Agency Partners—assesses the marketing agency ecosystem and shares systems for finding and managing marketing agency partners.

chapter 3

Build a Modern Marketing Team

The battle for top talent is brewing.

■ A TALENT WAR HAS BEGUN

A marketing talent war has begun for tech-savvy, hybrid marketers who are capable of building, managing, and executing fully integrated campaigns that produce measurable results. Businesses that have been slow to evolve do not know it yet, but the battle for top talent is brewing among forward-thinking agencies, publishers, corporations, and media companies.

These prototype marketers are able to deliver services across multiple marketing disciplines, including analytics, content, email, mobile, search, social, PR, and web. They are agile, adept at advanced marketing technologies, and experts at inbound strategy. Here is a peek at what hybrids are capable of doing to drive performance:

➤ Activate marketing automation tools, fully integrated with sales and CRM systems, to deliver maximum value at every consumer touchpoint.

➤ Analyze marketing data to turn information into intelligence and intelligence into action.

➤ Connect actions to outcomes.

➤ Create advanced buyer-persona profiles that serve as the foundation for highly personalized inbound marketing campaigns.

➤ Design marketing strategies around content consumption and buying patterns across multiple screens—including tablets, personal computers, and smartphones.

➤ Devise brand content calendars to match publishing schedules to buyer personas, web search trends, business milestones, and priority campaigns.

➤ Envision content, mobile apps, and online tools that create value for customers.

➤ Leverage advanced CMS technology to dynamically alter website copy and calls to action at an individual visitor level.

➤ Measure ROI by marketing channel to enable more sophisticated resource allocation.

➤ Personalize communications to speak to specific needs, pain points, and behavioral triggers.

➤ Prioritize and segment contact databases.

➤ Take a full-funnel approach, constructing marketing campaigns designed to achieve specific and measurable goals at every stage of the sales process.

➤ Stay immersed in marketing technology, trends, and social networks.

Transformation of a Traditional Marketer

In "Overcoming Extinction: 5 Tips to Stay Ahead of the Ever-Changing Marketing Curve,"[1] Anita Newton (@AnitaBNewton), vice president of corporate marketing at Adknowledge (@Adknowledge), shares a revealing story about her evolution as a marketer.

She recalls a time when she had to pull off a last-minute campaign on her own. "There I was, armed with campaign ideas, executive approval, and time earmarked to make it happen. The problem was, I didn't have the skills to make it happen: I didn't know how to set up a Facebook campaign, let alone a custom audience. I didn't have the knowledge to create a landing page, much less A/B test for success. I didn't even know where to start to send out a quick email to our subscriber list."

She writes, "I was a classically trained marketer who had cut my teeth at Procter & Gamble, negotiated multimillion-dollar deals with the NFL, and received an MBA at Harvard Business School. And I had become obsolete." Though she was only in her mid-30s, Newton realized she had already become "a fossil," dependent on managers, coordinators, agency partners, and digital associates to create brilliant marketing programs.

She made a choice then to take control of her career. Leaving the comfort zone of a large company, she joined a small startup, challenged herself to expand her skill sets, immersed herself in new technologies, and learned to build innovative strategies with marketing budgets a fraction of what she was used to when leading marketing at P&G, Sprint, and AMC Theaters.

In the time since, she has worked with and mentored dozens of startups, including Zave Networks (acquired by Google), and advised corporate executives and marketers on how to remain relevant in the rapidly changing marketing industry.

According to Newton, "Marketers now must, at the surface level, be able to master two sides of the same coin: First there is a rigorous focus on back to basics—connecting with customers, product/market fit, brand building, and customer development. But, on the other side, marketing has evolved into an analytically driven discipline. You have to be a brand marketer, but you also have to be a data scientist—and fully weave together these mindsets before deploying any new tool, tactic, or technology."[2]

Newton's transformation is a model for what is possible when marketers make the choice to adapt and evolve. Marketers do not have to become experts at everything, but they need to understand their weaknesses and continue expanding their knowledge and capabilities.

Anatomy of the Modern Marketing Team

So, what does a modern marketing team look like? What are the essential skills needed to build performance-driven businesses?

According to Accenture (@accenture), "Marketers will need to hire, reskill, and redeploy people to improve efficiency, agility, and responsiveness. Marketers need talent that can create consistent, multichannel experiences that meet customers' needs, expectations, and demands for relevance. Innovative employees are high on the CMO agenda. An emerging priority for marketing executives is to hire and grow talent that is digitally experienced and can integrate well with the IT department."[3]

Let's take a look at 15 core competencies that should be evaluated and integrated to varying levels based on your business's size, budgets, and goals. For SMBs, your team may primarily consist of outsourced agencies and consultants, which we will explore in Chapter 5. Large enterprises will likely have a mix of internal staff and outside partners.

Coding
While your company may not staff developers, your marketing team should make a point to grasp the basics of coding, which will help marketers understand what is possible when it comes to technology and communicate

better with their technical counterparts. In "7 Characteristics of Tomorrow's Best B2B Marketers," B2B digital blogger Eric Wittlake (@wittlake) states, "You don't need to be a developer or systems manager (yet), but databases, scripting languages and APIs should open the window of possibilities, not make your eyes glaze over."[4]

Check out www.TeamTreehouse.com for an affordable way to learn basic coding skills.

Copywriting

Content creation, and the ability to write persuasive copy for all marketing channels, is possibly the most important fundamental modern-marketing skill.

As discussed in Chapter 1, we have entered the age of content, context, and the customer experience. Brands have become storytellers, competing for the hearts and minds of consumers. Modern marketers create multimedia content to attract and engage audiences, and they use the context of consumer behavior to create personalized brand experiences.

The best copywriters use a blend of technical and creative writing skills to influence audiences. They understand the role of their writing in driving business results and are able to analyze and adapt their content based on performance. Effective business writing is strategic, brand-centric, buyer-persona focused, optimized for search engines, technically sound, creative, and results driven.

When building your team, keep in mind that while many modern-marketing skills can be taught postgraduate, copywriting is an art form that requires advanced training and repetition to perfect. Leading organizations will look to journalism schools for young professionals who can be molded into prototype marketers.

Data Analysis

There is a growing need to demonstrate marketing ROI and understand consumers' behavior through the context of their actions. Marketers must have strong analytical skills, specifically the ability to interpret website and marketing data, gauge campaign performance, and clearly communicate results to executives.

The deluge of data at marketers' fingertips gives them the ability to uncover actionable intelligence that can improve strategies, better target messaging, and drive bottom-line growth. However, according to IBM (@IBM), 71 percent of CMOs indicate that they are underprepared to manage the impact of this data explosion[5] and, according to CEB (@CEB_News), "on average, marketers depend on data for just 11 percent of customer-related decisions."[6]

This leaves tremendous untapped opportunities and potential for marketers who can effectively filter through the noise and uncover insight from data.

In his post "The Marketing Skills of the Future," author and speaker Christopher S. Penn (@cspenn) sums it up best: "The ability to be a data storyteller, to be someone who has the knowledge and experience to interpret data, is a valuable skill today, but as we increase the quantity of marketing data, it will become nearly priceless. Data is currently overwhelming; in the future, without analysis and insight, it'll become so unwieldy that it will be near useless."[7]

Email Marketing

Audience author Jeffrey K. Rohrs (@jkrohrs) defines proprietary audience development as "a comprehensive, collaborative, and cross-channel effort to build audiences that your company alone can access."

Marketing success is contingent on proprietary audience development, specifically the size and quality of your opt-in email database. According to Rohrs, "Proprietary audiences allow you to: (1) Reach CUSTOMERS and PROSPECTS at a lower cost. (2) Drive sales in a more on-demand fashion. (3) Treat consumers as individuals instead of faceless masses. (4) Optimize your budget across Paid, Owned, and Earned Media."[8]

Your marketing team must excel at building, reaching, and influencing proprietary audiences. Effective email marketers possess a deep understanding of buyer personas and the customer journey. They are able to segment and manage audience lists, develop personalized content, run automated email campaigns, provide insight into performance reports, and continually adapt activities to meet business goals.

If you are curious how your email marketing stacks up to the competition, MailChimp (@MailChimp), a leading email marketing provider, published an industry benchmarks report based on hundreds of millions of sent emails. The report tracked campaigns with more than 1,000 subscribers and companies ranging in size from one-person startups to Fortune 500 enterprises. The average open rate across 46 industries was 22.3 percent, and the average click-through rate was 3.2 percent.[9]

Event Planning

According to the 2014 "B2B Content Marketing" report from Content Marketing Institute (@CMIContent) and MarketingProfs (@MarketingProfs), "in-person events" are the most effective content marketing tactic, with a 70 percent effectiveness rating.[10]

So, while videos, blogs, webinars, podcasts, enewsletters, ebooks, and other digital content marketing activities are proven performance drivers, your business still needs to consider the impact of traditional events and offline networking.

How capable is your team at integrating business and networking events into your marketing strategy? If you do not have internal team members with event-planning capabilities, build connections with local vendors, venues, and professionals.

Graphic Design

Visual storytelling is critical, and strong graphic design skills are key to enhancing the value and shareability of your content marketing assets. As with coding, teams need to have either capabilities in-house or a trusted outside partner.

For businesses seeking affordable creative services, websites such as www.99Designs.com (@99designs) and www.crowdspring.com (@crowdSPRING) offer access to thousands of designers.

Lead Management

Marketers are being asked to drive actions and outcomes deeper into the marketing funnel. It is not enough to generate leads through a website, content downloads, events, and incoming phone calls. Now, marketers must score, nurture, and qualify leads before delivering them to sales. This requires that your team possess advanced capabilities with CRM and marketing automation technologies, which we will cover in depth in Chapters 6 and 7.

Mobile Strategy

According to Google's 2013 "Mobile Path to Purchase" report, 93 percent of people who use mobile to research products and services go on to make a purchase. Fifty-five percent of consumers researching on mobile intend to purchase within one hour, and 83 percent want to purchase within one day.[11]

Consumers are constantly connected through mobile. As smartphone and tablet usage soars, your team needs to be able to continually enhance its mobile strategy. Is your business showing up in mobile web searches? Does your website use responsive design to create a consistent brand experience? Should you be using a mobile app to engage audiences? These are important questions for your team to address.

Paid Media Management

Digital paid media is a highly measurable way to drive traffic, generate leads, and increase sales conversions. While proprietary audiences are the most affordable and effective to reach, marketers can amplify campaign messages through paid channels on social networks, search engines, blogs, websites, and third-party emails.

A modern marketing team needs professionals with a technical understanding of how paid media works and what opportunities exist to drive results through search, display ads, native content, and retargeting.

Public Relations

PR encompasses any activity, online or offline, designed to improve communications and build relationships. This includes, but is not limited to, analyst relations, blogger relations, community relations, crisis communications, employee relations, media relations, and public speaking.

Marketing professionals with PR skills are valued assets on a modern marketing team. Here is a sample of the activities they can use to drive performance:

➤ Leverage original content, including case studies, white papers, and ebooks, to generate media coverage.

➤ Monitor placements and mentions of the brand and organization leaders.

➤ Nurture relationships with writers, editors, bloggers, and analysts.

➤ Pursue editorial opportunities in media outlets.

➤ Place byline articles and guest blog posts.

➤ Secure speaking engagements and industry awards.

Search Engine Optimization (SEO)

Google, which controls approximately 67 percent of the search market,[12] answers more than 1 billion questions every day from people in 181 countries and in 146 languages.[13]

Ranking organically at the top of search engine results pages is a highly competitive and potentially lucrative endeavor for businesses. According to Compete.com (@compete), 53 percent of all organic clicks are on the first result, 15 percent are on the second, 9 percent on the third, 6 percent on the fourth, and 4 percent on the fifth.[14] So, if your business is not ranking at the top half of the first organic page for priority keywords, then your chances of being found are minimal.

Historically, SEO professionals focused on link building and keyword optimization to boost search rankings. However, in an effort to fight spam and protect user privacy, Google and other search engines have continued to evolve algorithms and reduce visibility into keyword performance. Specifically, in late 2013, Google began encrypting all nonpaid searches, which means marketers lost direct insight into the keywords visitors use to find their websites. Instead, "(not provided)" became the standard for referring organic traffic.

SEO, now more than ever, is about creating content and websites that users love and are willing to share. There are still indirect ways to gain insights into keyword searches and standard technical activities to optimize websites, but SEO strategies should largely be content strategies.

Focus your team on providing value, answering questions, and producing quality content.

Social Media

Social involves much more than sharing your content and building reach; it is an essential channel for increasing brand awareness, generating leads, nurturing prospects, connecting with peers, and engaging customers. Modern marketers are able to identify the social networks most relevant to their audiences and allocate resources to continually listen and engage.

When assessing your team's competencies, consider the following ways social can impact your business:

➤ Build stronger connections among employees, colleagues, and peers.

➤ Connect with existing customers in a more personal way.

➤ Connect with and nurture leads as part of the sales cycle.

➤ Develop strong personal brands for employees and leaders.

➤ Engage with influencers through social networks and blog commenting.

➤ Fill the job candidate pipeline with qualified professionals.

➤ Generate leads.

➤ Monitor mentions about the organization, leaders, and competitors.

➤ Share original content, including blog posts, ebooks, case studies, and videos.

➤ Raise the brand's profile within the industry.

➤ Stay on top of industry trends and news.

Strategic Planning

When building strategy, marketers must consider variables such as changes in content consumption and buying behaviors, a growing matrix of marketing technology solutions, the need for tighter integration with sales, and increased ROI expectations from the C-suite. Success requires what Altimeter Group (@altimetergroup) calls a "converged media" approach that mixes paid, owned, and earned media.[15]

➤ Paid media is advertising for which a media buy is necessary, including pay-per-click (PPC), display ads, sponsorships, and native content.

➤ Owned media is all content assets a brand either owns or wholly controls, including websites and blogs. Altimeter and Forrester both consider social media presence to be owned, but given that your ability to reach your followers and fans on those sites is controlled by third-party brands, I would classify some social connections as "borrowed."

➤ Earned media is user-generated content created and/or shared by users, such as social media posts, reviews, videos, photos, and open online communities. Online and offline mentions resulting from PR activities also fit under earned media.

➤ Converged media utilizes two or more channels of paid, earned, and owned media. It is characterized by a consistent story line, look, and feel. All channels work in concert, enabling brands to reach customers exactly where, how, and when they want, regardless of channel, medium, or device, online or offline.

Modern marketing teams are able to create a balanced mix of campaigns across channels. This requires a strong knowledge of paid media options and technology, an ability to build and maximize owned assets, and a savvy approach to earned media opportunities. Chapters 8 through 10 go in depth on marketing strategy.

Video Production

Consumers are creating and viewing online video in staggering numbers. More than 1 billion unique users visit YouTube each month, watching more than 6 billion hours of video per month.[16] According to Cisco (@cisco), online video traffic will account for 79 percent of all consumer Internet traffic by 2018.[17]

Does your team have the ability to strategize and produce video that connects with, entertains, and educates consumers?

Website Management

Your website is a lead-generation and multimedia content publishing tool. It gives your business the ability to gain insight into visitor behavior, create powerful customer experiences, build proprietary contact databases, and drive business growth.

Your team needs some technical skills to handle website development, design, and strategy, but CMS platforms have made it simple for any marketer with basic training to manage calls to action, content updates, landing pages, lead forms, and optimization.

The Marketing Organization Chart

As the marketing team evolves, traditional organization charts are becoming outdated. New models are emerging that are more customer-centric, but there is no cookie-cutter solution that fits every business. Your approach will depend on your products or services, industry, team size, and marketing goals.

Consider the following models as potential ways to segment teams and establish hierarchies.

➤ Customer life cycle stages (awareness, consideration, intent, decision, validation)

➤ Geographic regions (local, regional, national, international)

➤ Marketing goals (brand building, lead generation, sales, loyalty)

➤ Personas or industries

➤ Products or business categories

Keep in mind that some marketing functions may overlap with those of other departments. For example, social media engagement may be a joint effort between marketing and customer service. As you define your marketing structure, be sure to also establish open communication channels with other stakeholders across the company. Regardless of which model you choose, the key is to create a consistent customer experience, from first touchpoint through purchase and beyond.

See HubSpot CMO Mike Volpe's (@mvolpe) March 2014 presentation, "The CMO's Guide to Marketing Org Structure," for sample organizational charts from Forrester (@forrester), Rue La La (@RueLaLa), Mindjet (@Mindjet), GitHub (@github), HubSpot (@HubSpot), Zendesk (@Zendesk), and Atlassian (@atlassian).[18] The presentation is available on SlideShare at http://bit.ly/mkt-org-charts.

■ RISE OF THE HYBRIDS

Hybrid marketers can accelerate digital transformation and success within businesses, but, as we learned in Chapter 1, there is a growing talent gap, and marketers with advanced digital skill sets are in short supply.

Capgemini Consulting reports in its "Digital Talent Gap" study that 90 percent of companies lack necessary digital skills in key areas of social media, mobile, internal social networks, process automation, and performance monitoring and analysis.[19]

According to WANTED Analytics (@WANTEDAnalytics), a provider of business intelligence for the talent marketplace, digital advertising and marketing jobs saw a 19 percent year-over-year increase in 2013, with the most commonly required skills being digital marketing, online advertising, SEO, marketing strategy, CRM, marketing communications, and integrated marketing. However, looking at WANTED Analytics' Hiring Scale, digital marketing positions rate an 86 on a 1-to-99 scale, with 99 representing the most hard-to-fill conditions.[20]

Businesses must compete for the limited number of qualified digital-savvy marketing professionals while building strategies to discover and nurture candidates with A-player potential from diverse educational backgrounds.

The best marketers likely have jobs, so attracting experienced high performers requires a commitment to creating a sought-after work environment and having a strategy focused on engaging candidates over the long term. You never know when A players will be in the market for more creative freedom, greater resources, higher profile opportunities, or the chance to challenge themselves in new ways. Your brand has to be top of mind when that time comes.

The same thinking applies to entry-level professionals. As we will see in Chapter 4, universities are falling behind industry demand for digital marketing talent. The most motivated and advanced students will have their choice of career paths, so businesses must take a more sophisticated approach to discovering and nurturing candidates. When hiring straight out of college, look for young professionals whose education, core skill sets, and personality traits set them apart. Specifically, consider these eight traits:

1. **Analytical:** They crave knowledge to understand cause and effect. They use data to gain insight, determine strategy, and build support.

2. **Creative:** They think outside the box and move beyond the tried and true to discover innovative strategies that can propel businesses forward. Test for creativity in the interview process, and look at past work for signs of innovative thinking.

3. **Intrinsically motivated:** They derive fulfillment from being a part of something greater than themselves. They do not define success by money, fame, or power, but rather by the pursuit of purpose. The intrinsically motivated challenge authority, seek autonomy and flexibility, desire balance, and value the freedom to pursue passions outside their careers.

4. **Attentive:** They listen closely, take notes, maintain strong eye contact in conversations, avoid distractions, and process information before making decisions.

5. **Social-web savvy:** They monitor and participate in social networks relevant to their interests and the industry. They become a part of the conversation.

6. **Strategic:** They are capable of seeing the big picture and connecting seemingly unrelated things. They always understand how tactical elements play into one another, and they measure everything.

7. **Tech-savvy:** They research and test what is new and what is next. They stay informed on emerging technologies and consider applications to their businesses and careers.

8. **Collaborative:** They know that team comes first and look for opportunities to advance their peers and the company. Egos can undermine success.

The reality is that most businesses will struggle to find polished digital marketers at any level with the array of experience and knowledge needed to excel. So, your company's future success will depend on your ability to identify potential and develop your own team of hybrids through internal education programs (see Chapter 4).

■ THE SCIENCE OF RECRUITING

What can your organization do to attract talent now? In short, think like modern marketers, and put inbound marketing strategy and technology to work.

Author and consultant Heather R. Huhman (@heatherhuhman) sums it up best: "Companies and organizations are beginning to realize the battle for finding the best modern marketing talent. Tech-savvy, modern marketers excel in digital marketing strategies such as creating content, analytics, and social media. If you want to find these professionals, then you have to have a modern recruiting strategy."[21]

Step 1: Map Skills Gaps

Start by identifying the skills needed for a modern marketing team, and then rate your staff and agency partners. Earlier in this chapter, we identified 15 skills and eight core traits that can serve as a starting point for your assessment.

Step 2: Define Candidate Personas

Profile career candidates the same way you would buyer personas. Ask yourself:

➤ What matters to them when researching career options?

➤ Where do they go for information and resources?

➤ What are their primary concerns and questions?

➤ What is their educational background and career experience?

➤ How do they evaluate companies?

➤ What do they value, and how do they make career decisions?

Step 3: Adjust Brand Positioning

Think of your business as a career destination, not a stepping-stone. HubSpot's "Culture Code," which has more than 1.3 million Slideshare views as of June 2014, is a great example of positioning a brand to attract talent.[22]

Intrinsically motivated professionals, who are essential to your success, value companies and careers with purpose. Think about culture and what your business has to offer outside of compensation.

Step 4: Create Candidate-Focused Content

Are you publishing blog posts, ebooks, photos, videos, and more targeted at career candidates? If not, you should be. These content assets are the ideal way to tell your company story and engage prospective employees in your brand.

Work with HR to identify content and resources that would be valuable to candidate personas, and then build those assets into the content marketing editorial calendar.

Step 5: Build Landing Pages with Profiling Questions

Shift away from the standard online forms and job listings, and use landing pages with lead forms to capture candidates. The forms should be tied to a back-end CRM or application management system that maintains updated records for each candidate.

For example, at PR 20/20, we use landing pages and forms to gather inbound candidates. This gives us greater insight into candidates and the ability to connect their responses to CRM contact records for scoring and nurturing.

Which leads us to the next step.

Step 6: Score and Segment Candidates Using Behavior-Based Signals

Once you gather profile information, you can activate a candidate scoring system (similar to how you would set up lead scoring), which gives preference, or greater weight, to specific skills, education, and experience.

But do not stop there.

By integrating marketing technology into your recruiting process, you can use behavior-based signals to impact candidates' overall ratings. Did they view the "about" page? Did they click on the "careers" page recommended reading links?

Segment the most engaged candidates into priority lists, and move on to step 7.

Step 7: Activate Automated Email Workflows

Nurture your career candidates. Use marketing technology to set up automated emails that provide them with valuable resources, and offer additional touchpoints to monitor their engagement and interest.

The candidate-focused content you created in step 4 fuels the nurturing emails. Watch open and click rates, and be sure that you have accounted for these interactions in your candidate scoring formula.

Your best candidates are going to be the professionals who meet the obvious skill/education/experience requirements but who also demonstrate a desire to continually advance their knowledge and capabilities and engage with your brand.

By applying inbound marketing strategy and technology to your recruiting process, you will give your organization a distinct advantage when competing for top marketing talent.

CHAPTER HIGHLIGHTS

➤ A marketing talent war has begun for tech-savvy, hybrid marketers who are capable of building, managing, and executing fully integrated campaigns that produce measurable results.

(*continued*)

➤ Hybrids are agile, adept at advanced marketing technologies, and expert at inbound strategy.

➤ While your company may not staff developers, your marketing team should make a point to grasp the basics of coding, which will help marketers understand what is possible when it comes to technology and communicate better with their technical counterparts.

➤ Content creation, and the ability to write persuasive copy for all marketing channels, is possibly the most important fundamental modern-marketing skill.

➤ Marketers must have strong analytical skills, specifically the ability to interpret website and marketing data, gauge campaign performance, and clearly communicate results to executives.

➤ Marketing success is contingent on proprietary audience development, specifically the size and quality of your opt-in email database.

➤ Marketers need a technical understanding of how paid search programs work and what opportunities exist to drive results through paid search, display ads, native content, and retargeting.

➤ SEO, now more than ever, is about creating content and websites that users love and are willing to share.

➤ When building inbound strategy, marketers must consider variables such as changes in content consumption and buying behaviors, a growing matrix of marketing technology solutions, the need for tighter integration with sales, and increased ROI expectations from the C-suite.

➤ Businesses must compete for the limited number of qualified digital-savvy inbound marketing professionals while building strategies to discover and nurture candidates with A-player potential from diverse educational backgrounds.

➤ To attract top talent, think like modern marketers and put inbound marketing strategy and technology to work.

chapter 4

Construct an Internal Marketing Academy

Businesses must take the initiative to mold their own modern marketers.

■ KEEPING PACE OR FALLING BEHIND?

As demand for performance-driven, digital-savvy talent rises, universities are struggling to prepare students for the reality of a rapidly changing industry. Courses in analytics, automation, content, email, mobile, social, and other critical areas are rarely deeply integrated into marketing programs.

While digital-related courses are commonly offered as electives, our research of the top 10 undergraduate marketing programs in the United States, according to the 2014 *U.S. News & World Report* rankings,[1] showed only one, Indiana University Bloomington (@IUBloomington), has a required digital marketing course—Analysis of Marketing Data.

College students generally have opportunities to learn digital marketing strategy and tactics. However, because of the way the higher education system is structured, many can earn undergraduate marketing degrees without taking a single digital class.

In "Will Universities Evolve?" Rand Schulman (@randschulman), executive-in-residence for new media/marketing at University of the Pacific (@UOPacific), states, "U.S. universities are not adequately training students to meet the needs of business in some of the most sought-after areas of marketing: social media, content marketing and content analytics. Clearly an imbalance exists between skills taught in classrooms and the skills sought in the marketplace—and this imbalance is only accelerating by the rapid pace of change in technology and product innovation... too few marketing students are given rigorous, cross-disciplinary training in writing, analytics and technology."[2]

But is it realistic to expect universities to keep up?

According to marketing author and business consultant Mark Schaefer (@markwschaefer), who is also an adjunct marketing professor at Rutgers University (@RutgersU), "Right now, the university system is structured and rewarded for stability, with an emphasis on long-term research." This system, he notes, works very well for disciplines such as English literature, finance, and accounting—but fails in the rapidly evolving fields of marketing, advertising, public relations, and marketing communications.

Schaefer points out that in digital marketing, and particularly social media marketing, "Not only are the platforms dynamic, but the rules of engagement are dynamic." Competitive candidates must "not just be trained, but immersed" in digital marketing tools and technologies.[3]

And thus, we arrive at the crux of the higher education issue. Change velocity within the marketing industry is unparalleled in history and is gaining momentum. Without dramatic shifts to the overall higher education system, it is unlikely that academia will be able to keep pace.

Outliers and Innovators

While higher education as a whole is behind the digital marketing transformation curve, there are outliers making tremendous efforts to advance their students.

Academic innovators include professors and administrators with a sense of urgency to adapt curriculum and course materials. They are keenly aware of the skills marketing professionals need and realize they must continually immerse their students in marketing technologies and trends. Students are prepared with the strategic decision-making skills to adjust to an ever-evolving landscape, while being given opportunities to apply critical thinking skills to real-world challenges.

That is exactly what is happening at Ball State University (@BallState) in Muncie, Indiana. Jeffrey L. Cohen (@jeffreylcohen) joined the university in January 2014 as a distinguished lecturer in marketing analytics and social media. Cohen is a marketing veteran and a leading social media blogger who led the content marketing team for Salesforce.com. His social media marketing and web analytics classes contain a mix of theory and practice and give students a hands-on, immersive experience by working with clients and using the latest tools.

"I've built the class framework in such a way that the major topics form the spine of the content," says Cohen, "but we talk about current social media examples, new platforms, and the latest data. I have practitioners join the class by videoconference to add a real-world perspective, and I continue to speak at marketing industry conferences, consult with clients, and interview industry leaders about the latest developments. This keeps the curriculum fresh and relevant."[4]

Schaefer suggests that universities must find a way around their own barriers. For example, Rutgers University has developed a highly regarded program outside the standard accreditation process. Content and classes, which are taught by nationally renowned marketing practitioners, flex as needed to focus on timely marketing topics. The week-long seminars offer open enrollment to university students as well as nonstudents. Participants can earn college credits, continuing education credits, or certifications.

■ THE ROLE OF ONLINE EDUCATION

In his June 2013 TED talk, Anant Agarwal (@agarwaledu), MIT (@MIT) professor and edX (@edXOnline) CEO, stated, "Education really hasn't changed in the last 500 years. The last big innovation in education was the printing press and the textbooks."[5]

However, in the last few years, the education industry experienced the rapid ascent of MOOCs, or massive open online courses, which challenged the status quo. In spring 2012, Agarwal taught an online course called Circuits and Electronics. The course enrolled 155,000 students from 162 countries, with 7,200 students passing the course. This was the inaugural offering of what became edX, an online venture of MIT and Harvard (@Harvard) with nearly 2 million students. Coursera (@coursera), the leading MOOC provider, has more than 6 million registered students worldwide as of February 2014.

While the success of MOOCs has been called into question due to low completion rates, there is no denying their disruptive potential within an archaic higher-learning system. Future adjustments to improve MOOCs' performance will likely center around personalization and adaptive learning at an individual student level rather than the one-to-many model.

In "The Attack on Our Higher Education System—And Why We Should Welcome It," George Siemens (@gsiemens) writes, "What learners really need has diversified over the past several decades as the knowledge economy has expanded. Universities have not kept pace with learner needs and MOOCs have caused a much needed stir—a period of reflection and self-assessment. To date, higher education has largely failed to learn the lessons of participatory culture, distributed and fragmented value systems and networked learning. MOOCs have forced a serious assessment of the idea of a university and how education should be related to and supportive of the society in which it exists."[6]

Demand for online courses has proven the market for continued investment and innovation in the space. Privately funded and venture-backed organizations are stepping up to deliver continuing education and certification in digital marketing. Here is a look at eight companies providing education, training, and certification critical to producing modern marketers. This is by no means a complete list of available programs, but these companies offer a solid starting point for marketers.

1. **Codecademy** (@Codecademy): More than 24 million unique users have signed up to take free coding classes. The company, which is backed by some of the most prominent venture capital firms in the world, gives marketers the ability to learn popular programming languages, including HTML, CSS, jQuery, JavaScript, PHP, Python, and Ruby. www.Codecademy.com

2. **Content Marketing Institute** (@CMIContent): The Content Marketing Institute launched its Online Training and Certification program in March 2014 with 35 lessons and more than 18 hours of training. Courses are taught by industry experts and designed to help marketers build a strong foundation for content marketing efforts in seven key areas: planning, audience, story, channels, process, conversation, and measurement. www.ContentMarketingInstitute.com

3. **Google** (@Google): The Google Analytics Academy is a free online learning platform that offers comprehensive training in Google Analytics and data analysis. In addition, the help center has video lessons on analytics that prepare you for the Google Analytics Individual Qualification (IQ) test. www.Google.com/analytics/learn/

4. **HubSpot** (@HubSpot): HubSpot is an example of a marketing software company investing in education and training as a means to advance the industry, generate new business leads, and create more successful and loyal customers. HubSpot's inbound certification includes online classes that cover the core elements of the inbound methodology, from optimizing websites to landing page anatomy to segmenting contact databases. HubSpot also offers product and marketing agency partner certifications. http://Academy.Hubspot.com

5. **MarketingProfs** (@MarketingProfs): Trusted by more than 620,000 professionals worldwide, MarketingProfs provides "Real-World Education for Modern Marketers." Founded in 2000, MarketingProfs delivers online training in branding, content marketing, digital marketing, email marketing, lead generation and nurturing, marketing writing, mobile marketing, online advertising, social media marketing, and more. Its Enterprise Pro+ program includes a customizable learning center, online courses, interactive seminars, reporting, and metrics, as well as an online library with more than 6,500 resources. Professionals can also earn certifications through the MarketingProfs University program. www.MarketingProfs.com

6. **Online Marketing Institute** (@OMInstitute): Founded in 2007, the Online Marketing Institute (OMI) hosts an online library of more than 100

digital marketing classes taught by leading practitioners. OMI offers online classes in social media marketing, digital marketing, email, analytics, and B2B marketing. Online crash courses discuss the latest trends and best practices in digital marketing, while online summits teach digital marketing over a three-day period. OMI also provides self-paced online certification programs. www.OnlineMarketingInstitute.org

7. **Treehouse** (@treehouse): Treehouse hosts more than 1,000 videos on web design, coding, and business basics. More than 59,000 professionals and businesses have used Treehouse's interactive learning system, which includes quizzes and challenges to test knowledge and rewards achievements with badges and points. Businesses can create groups and then monitor team standings to add an element of gamification to the learning process. www.TeamTreehouse.com

8. **Udemy** (@udemy): More than 2 million students in more than 190 countries take online courses on Udemy.com. A search on Udemy for "marketing" produced more than 200 free and paid courses. Each course is designed and taught by an expert instructor, and hundreds of new courses are published every month. Udemy for Organizations (UFO) offers two corporate learning solutions that let you build private and secure training libraries. Users can select from existing Udemy courses and add their own internal content using the course creation tool. www.Udemy.com

■ AN INTERNAL ACADEMY MODEL

For businesses looking to build a team of modern marketers, online education platforms offer incredible access to an almost endless array of courses and certifications. Rather than relying on undergraduate and graduate programs to produce digital-savvy professionals, businesses can tap into the wealth of content and experts available online to build their own internal academies.

Universities still play an instrumental role in preparing students for professional marketing careers, but for the foreseeable future, businesses must take the initiative to mold their own modern marketers. High-performing companies find candidates at all levels with the necessary core competencies and traits (strong writing abilities, detail-oriented, analytical, strategic, curious, intrinsically motivated), train them through a blend of internal and external resources, and immerse them in marketing technology and strategy.

According to the Online Marketing Institute, only 28 percent of large enterprises plan to introduce formal training programs to improve digital marketing skills, so the opportunity exists for businesses, large and small, to create a competitive advantage through talent.[7]

Whether you are constructing a new marketing team from scratch or evolving the skills and capabilities of your existing staff, following are 11 steps to consider when building your internal marketing academy. There are enterprise-level learning management systems you can implement to devise large-scale programs, but most organizations can run effective initiatives with spreadsheets, email, and project management software.

Step 1: Appoint an Academy Leader

Install an academy leader who will champion the program with internal stakeholders and function as the project manager to facilitate all planning and activation. In large enterprises, this is likely a human resource function, but in SMBs, look for a team member who understands the significance of digital transformation to the organization and who wants to play an integral role in moving your marketing forward.

Step 2: Define Academy Goals

The academy must have clear goals to win executive support and employee buy-in. Start with the "why." Why are you creating an internal academy? How do academy goals tie to the overall marketing strategy, and how do they support achievement of business and personal career goals?

According to Capgemini Consulting's ebook, *The Digital Talent Gap: Developing Skills for Today's Digital Organizations*, only 4 percent of companies studied ensured their training efforts were aligned with overall digital strategy.[8] Do not make the same mistake. For example, if your business has strong brand awareness and excels at driving website traffic and building reach, yet struggles at all aspects of lead generation and nurturing, then one academy goal may be to enhance lead-generation skills and technology usage. You can measure improvement by establishing benchmarks in an up-front skills assessment.

Step 3: Conduct a Skills Assessment

Once you have identified the skills critical for marketing success, develop an assessment to rate your current and future marketers. An overall team rating is a good starting point, but you will want to perform assessments at an individual level to identify team members' strengths and weaknesses. This helps guide curriculum and construct personalized development plans.

Assessments also assist in determining the need for outsourced services from agencies and consultants, which we cover in Chapter 5. For example, if you have an outside agency that handles all your coding and mobile and you have no intention of bringing those skills in-house, then those areas will not be high priority when you build your curriculum.

MARKETING TEAM SKILLS ASSESSMENT

Marketing Skills	Pro 1	Pro 2	Pro 3	Pro 4	Pro 5	Skill Average
Coding						
Copywriting						
Data Analysis						
Email Marketing						
Event Planning						
Graphic Design						
Lead Management						
Mobile Strategy						
Paid Media Management						
Public Relations						
Search Engine Optimization						
Social Media						
Strategic Planning						
Video Production						
Website Management						
Pro Average						

Figure 4.1   Sample Skills Assessment

See Figure 4.1 for a sample assessment spreadsheet.

[+] A template skills assessment spreadsheet is available for download in the Marketing Performance Pack. Visit performance.PR2020.com.

Step 4: Build the Curriculum

Use a mix of internal training and exercises, combined with third-party resources, to compile your academy curriculum. You can easily manage recommended and required coursework through a Google Sheet or Excel file. This allows your academy leader to monitor progress at an individual professional level while seeing the big picture of how the team is developing as a whole.

Potential curriculum components include the following:

➤ **Online courses:** In the previous section, we looked at organizations offering online courses that can be integrated into internal academies. You can start with the eight featured examples, then expand your curriculum to include content from companies and experts most relevant to your needs, industries, and goals.

➤ **Industry certifications:** Tapping into existing industry programs is an efficient way to ensure your marketers advance their knowledge and apply newfound skills to earn certifications. For example, we require all PR 20/20 (@pr2020) professionals to pass the Google Analytics Individual Qualification (IQ) exam and complete HubSpot inbound and product certifications.

➤ **Conferences:** Some of the most valuable digital marketing education happens offline at industry conferences around the world. Content Marketing World (@CMIContent), IBM Connect (@IBMConnect), INBOUND (@HubSpot), MarTech (@martechconf), Pubcon (@pubcon), and SXSW Interactive (@sxsw) are some of the top events to consider as part of your ongoing education initiative.

➤ **Books:** Maintain a shared list of recommended and required reading as part of the academy, and keep track of which books each marketer has read. Ideally, have marketers rate books and offer comments and notes to give other team members some additional perspective. A few of my current marketing favorites include *Audience* by Jeffrey K. Rohrs (@jkrohrs), *Brandscaping* by Andrew Davis (@TPLDrew), *Ctrl Alt Delete* by Mitch Joel (@mitchjoel), *Epic Content Marketing* by Joe Pulizzi (@JoePulizzi), *The New Rules of Marketing & PR* by David Meerman Scott (@dmscott), and *Youtility* by Jay Baer (@jaybaer).

➤ **Webinars:** Webinars are everywhere. Software companies, marketing agencies, analyst firms, online institutes, publishers, and businesses across pretty much every industry are using free and paid webinars to educate audiences and drive business growth. There is a lot of noise and low-quality content out there, but there are also some gems that can enhance the value of your internal academy.

➤ **Internal topic experts:** Feature your own internal experts. From executives and sales leaders to engineers and customer service representatives, there is a wealth of knowledge and experience within your organization. Seek unique perspectives to broaden your marketers' understanding of the business, the industry, and the customer. Be sure to capture video recordings of internal expert presentations for future use.

➤ **Guest lecturers:** If your organization has strong connections with industry thought leaders, including analysts, authors, media contacts, and practitioners, invite them to present timely topics to your team. As with your internal experts, if you receive permission, record guest lecturer sessions for on-demand access.

➤ **Exercises:** Give marketers the opportunity to apply their learning with real-world exercises. For example, one of our senior consultants, Keith Moehring (@keithmoehring), created a Google Wizardry 101 program to advance the team's analytical and strategic thinking skills. He provides a challenge using actual data from Google Analytics, then professionals are allotted time to log into the account and present their findings and recommendations. Exercises like this are a great way to engage the team in learning and continually reinforce core knowledge and skills.

➤ **Knowledge transfer:** Document and store best practices, case studies, templates, demonstration videos, policies, and processes. Make it easy for marketers to access assets that streamline learning and expand their knowledge base. Internal social networks, such as Yammer (@Yammer) and Jive (@JiveSoftware), are a great way to share knowledge and resources for real-time learning. We use Yammer at PR 20/20 to post links, ask questions, seek feedback, and recommend educational resources. Think about ways you can use an internal social network as part of your academy to enhance knowledge transfer.

Step 5: Map Standard Paths

Once you have conducted the skills assessment and built the academy curriculum, it is time to map learning paths featuring a collection of tracks and courses with associated timelines. Common ways to structure paths are by career stage, skill set, and performance goals. For example:

> ➤ **Foundations track:** Ideal for onboarding new marketers and outside partners, a foundations track may offer courses in digital marketing principles, proprietary processes, core technologies, business and industry fundamentals, historical marketing performance, marketing strategy, and priority certifications.

> ➤ **Analytics track:** Marketers must be able to turn data into intelligence, intelligence into actions, and actions into outcomes. An analytics track could feature advanced Google Analytics training and a collection of ongoing internal workshops.

> ➤ **Lead generation track:** Marketers are taking on greater responsibility for lead generation and lead quality. A lead generation track may include an introduction to marketing automation, content strategy, social selling, analytics basics, sales integration, and website management.

Step 6: Personalize Individual Assessment Plans

Standard paths lay the framework, but personalized advancement plans optimize the learning experience. Individual plans take into account strengths and weaknesses identified in the skills assessment, roles and responsibilities, career paths, performance goals, and unique learning styles.

Modern marketing talent may be your greatest asset and competitive advantage. Take the time to tailor the approach on an individual professional level.

Step 7: Establish a Feedback Loop

Encourage your team to share concerns, questions, and ideas. Use surveys and open forums to gain valuable feedback on the curriculum, and constantly look for ways to improve the academy, increase engagement, and drive performance.

Step 8: Develop Support Systems

Consider adding a mentor program to nurture professionals along their designated learning paths. For entry-level professionals, adjusting to the real-world pace, along with managing ongoing education requirements, can be daunting. Mentors help to ease the transition and provide much-needed guidance as they adapt. The same can be true of traditional marketers who are faced with evolution or obsolescence. Mentors can serve as confidants, supporters, and companions to keep teammates motivated and focused.

Group learning is another great way to provide support systems for team members going through the same training and certifications. For example, form an internal marketing book club to read and discuss a new marketing or business book each month.

Step 9: Automate Management Emails

Schedule regular emails to remind professionals of training milestones, and provide recommended resources to continually advance their knowledge and capabilities. At PR 20/20, we use our marketing automation software to streamline the process. For example, when a new employee is hired, we activate an automated email workflow that sends prewritten messages at regular intervals. Each email contains upcoming training milestone reminders, along with relevant resources.

Step 10: Create a Measurement and Recognition System

Everyone loves to see and feel progress. Points and badges are common ways to measure and recognize achievements as your team advances through the academy. Consider assigning standard point values to each activity in your curriculum. Points can be used to set professional development goals, monitor individual efforts, and compare individuals against their peers. Treehouse, which was featured earlier in this chapter, is a great example of how to apply points to your training and education program.

Step 11: Conduct Performance Reviews

Internal academies, like marketing campaigns, must produce an ROI. Integrate professional development efforts into employee performance reviews, and, ideally, tie professional development to career advancement and compensation. The skills assessment in step 3 establishes competency benchmarks, and the point system from step 10 provides a quantifiable means to measure and monitor progress.

CHAPTER HIGHLIGHTS

➤ As demand for performance-driven, digital-savvy talent rises, universities are struggling to prepare students for the reality of a rapidly changing industry.

(continued)

➤ While higher education as a whole is behind the digital marketing transformation curve, there are outliers making tremendous efforts to advance their students.

➤ Future adjustments to improve MOOCs' performance will likely center around personalization and adaptive learning at an individual student level rather than the one-to-many model.

➤ Demand for online courses has proven the market for continued investment and innovation in the space.

➤ Businesses can tap into the wealth of content and experts available online to build their own internal academies.

➤ High-performing businesses find candidates at all levels with the necessary core competencies and traits (strong writing abilities, detail-oriented, analytical, strategic, curious, intrinsically motivated), train them through a blend of internal and external resources, and immerse them in marketing technology and strategy.

➤ The opportunity exists for businesses, large and small, to create a competitive advantage through talent.

➤ Standard education paths lay the framework, but personalized advancement plans optimize the learning experience. Individual plans take into account strengths and weaknesses identified in the skills assessment, roles and responsibilities, career paths, performance goals, and unique learning styles.

➤ Internal academies, like marketing campaigns, must produce an ROI.

chapter 5

Propel Growth through Agency Partners

The marketing industry is moving too fast to internalize everything.

■ THE MARKETING AGENCY ECOSYSTEM

The marketing services industry is in a state of flux. As CMOs navigate the marketing talent gap, they are increasingly seeking performance-driven agency partners that are immersed in marketing technology and staffed with digital-savvy professionals. SMBs need partners that can deliver fully integrated solutions and in essence function as outsourced inbound marketing teams. Large enterprises commonly look for niche expertise in core digital disciplines such as content marketing, paid search, SEO, social media monitoring, and analytics to complement internal marketing teams.

The future belongs to dynamic agencies with more efficient management systems, integrated services, versatile talent, value-based pricing models, a love for data, and a commitment to producing measurable results. These tech-savvy modern marketing firms thrive on change and continually apply advances in technology to strengthen their businesses, adapt their services, and deliver greater value to you, the client.

As I wrote in my first book, *The Marketing Agency Blueprint*, "We are on the cusp of a truly transformational period in the marketing-services industry. The old guard, rooted in tradition and resistant to change, will fall and new leaders will emerge. The industry will be redefined by marketing agencies that are more nimble, tech savvy, open, and collaborative. Digital services will be ingrained into the DNA of every agency, and blended with traditional methods to execute integrated campaigns.... Their value and success will be measured by outcomes, not outputs."[1]

However, these digital-savvy firms are in short supply. Online education and certification initiatives, such as those discussed in Chapter 4, are building a more advanced ecosystem of marketing service providers. But for the time being, the agency landscape remains littered with traditional agencies struggling to transform their archaic business models. The traditionalists that are unable or unwilling to evolve will eventually fade, and the new category of disruptive agencies will rise to prominence.

But this disrupting class will take time to mature and will struggle to scale growth and meet demand in the short term.

■ FINDING YOUR MATCH

Despite the challenges of finding digital-savvy agency partners, marketers are outsourcing at record rates. According to Accenture's "Turbulence for the CMO" report, CMOs are turning to a large mix of agency partners and marketing service providers, outsourcing "between 45 percent and 75 percent of marketing activities." Paid search (41 percent), search engine optimization (39 percent), social media monitoring (37 percent), email marketing

(33 percent), web analytics (32 percent), marketing analytics (30 percent), and marketing automation (28 percent) are among the digital activities being farmed out to integrated agencies and specialty shops.[2]

The Accenture study, which surveyed 405 senior executives, mostly with at least $1 billion in annual revenue, reports that "CMOs are generally more satisfied with marketing areas managed by external resources than with their own people."

However, other studies, including "More Strain, Less Gain" from the CMO Council (@CMO_Council) and Ace Metrix (@Ace_Metrix), report that marketers still face an uphill battle in connecting agency activities to performance metrics. In the press release introducing the 2012 report, Donovan Neale-May, CMO Council executive director, states, "There's an underlying level of frustration among senior corporate marketers worldwide when it comes to agency contributions to business value creation, strategic thinking, and digital marketing development."[3]

The right marketing agency can be a tremendous asset to your organization and play a critical role in propelling growth, but marketers must take a methodical approach to finding the right firms. Here are seven rules to keep in mind when evaluating and selecting agency partners.

1. Partner with Performance-Driven Firms

Marketers are being held to higher ROI standards, and the same needs to be true of agency partners. Historically, marketing agencies have gotten away with reporting relatively meaningless metrics such as impressions, advertising equivalency, and PR value, or relying strictly on qualitative results.

Leading marketing agencies build campaigns that consistently produce measurable outcomes, including website traffic, subscribers, leads, and sales. Work with agency partners that care as much about performance and success as you do.

2. Assess the Account Team

The greatest value an agency can bring a client is staffing its account team with A players. Look for firms that have a history of recruiting and retaining top talent.

Understand how your account team will be structured, including who is responsible for planning, production, account management, and day-to-day client communications. Also consider if the firm you hire is outsourcing any services to freelancers or partner agencies. This is a common practice, but it is important that you are aware of and have confidence in any third parties that will be working on your account.

3. Find Tech-Savvy Firms

Agencies whose professionals are immersed in technology trends and innovations are able to more readily adapt their own business models, continually increase productivity, evolve client campaigns, and make strategic connections to seemingly unrelated information.

Find out what marketing technologies the agency uses to run its own business, how it integrates technology into client campaigns, and how it ensures that its staff remains current on technology news and trends.

4. Demand That Digital Is Ingrained in Their DNA

Every agency that will be relevant in the future is a digital agency. Having a digital division or group within a traditional agency is not sufficient. Digital has to be ingrained into the agency's culture and talent.

Agencies structured in service-area silos—social, search, mobile, web, email, analytics—will face the same challenges as their corporate counterparts when trying to build digital marketing strategies and campaigns. Digital must be fully integrated, along with traditional activities, into every program and budget.

5. Invest in the Doers

The marketing services world is full of thinkers, talkers, and self-proclaimed gurus. Turn to agencies with demonstrated track records of success, starting with their own brands. Evaluate the strength of their website, the power of their staff's personal brands, the value and frequency of content on their blog, and their reach and engagement in social networks.

6. Seek Systems for Success

Prototype agencies are powered by systems that continually increase efficiencies and productivity, encourage creativity and innovation, and push professionals to realize and embrace their potential. All of this produces higher performance levels and more satisfied clients.

Align your organization with agencies that take a systemic approach to professional development, project management, client services, monitoring, measurement, reporting, and communications. These firms:

➤ Keep projects on time and in budget.

➤ Maintain high levels of attention to detail and quality.

➤ Set realistic expectations and goals, which align with client resources and potential.

➤ Communicate project statuses, campaign successes and setbacks, shifts in priorities, real-time opportunities, and more.

➤ Produce measurable results.

7. Find Partners, Not Providers

Marketing agencies often look and sound the same. They offer similar services, tout impressive client lists, and flaunt industry awards lauding their creativity. But none of that really matters to your business. When selecting an agency partner, it is essential to move beyond the standard stuff and find partners who think and act differently and take a customized approach to your business.

When all else is equal, it is an agency's culture and talent that determine its ability to positively impact your business. We have found that the most successful marketing programs are those built on strong client-agency partnerships with a foundation of trust, respect, and aligned expectations and goals. These are the relationships in which the client looks to the agency as an extension of its marketing team, not as just another vendor.

Your agency team has to become indispensible through their hard work, insight, consultation, services, expertise, friendship, and professionalism. They must do the little things that build relationships and take the time to show you they care about your successes, both on individual and organizational levels.

Turn to Partner Programs and Marketplaces

Online service-provider marketplaces, agency match networks, and marketing technology company partner programs offer marketers a starting point when searching for modern marketing agencies.

If you are using a marketing automation solution, such as Act-On (@ActOnSoftware), Eloqua (@Eloqua), HubSpot (@HubSpot), Infusionsoft (@Infusionsoft), Marketo (@marketo), or Pardot (@Pardot), begin your search with their certified agency programs. These vetted partners will be the most educated and advanced users of the marketing technologies that are essential to your success.

If you are looking for specialized support in content or design, there are a number of online marketplaces built to help find qualified service providers. All funding information shown for the following marketplace companies is via www.crunchbase.com and is accurate as of March 2014.

➤ **99designs** (@99designs): 99designs is an online graphic design marketplace connecting startups, small businesses, marketing agencies, and other organizations with more than 250,000 graphic designers from 192 countries. The company raised $35 million in Series A funding in 2011.[4]
www.99designs.com

➤ **Contently** (@contently): Contently is a marketplace that connects journalists with publishers to help brands tell great stories. Contently builds software to help each party succeed in its goals: editorial management and content marketing software for publishers, personal branding and job-finding tools for journalists. The company closed a Series B financing round in January 2014, bringing its funding total to $12 million.[5]
www.contently.com

➤ **crowdSPRING** (@crowdSPRING): crowdSPRING is an online marketplace founded to help people around the world access creative talent and to help marketing professionals find new customers. The site features logo design; web design; company name, product name, and packaging design; and many other graphic design, industrial design, and writing services. There are more than 150,000 designers and writers in the marketplace. crowdSPRING raised $3 million in angel funding in 2008.[6]
www.crowdspring.com

➤ **DesignCrowd** (@DesignCrowd): DesignCrowd is an online marketplace providing custom logo, website, print, and graphic design services in 40 categories from more than 150,000 designers. The Australia-based company has raised $6.3 million since 2009.[7]
www.designcrowd.com

➤ **Scripted** (@getscripted): Scripted is an online marketplace that matches freelance writers with small businesses seeking blog posts, website content, white papers, social media updates, email newsletters, press releases, and video scripts. The company has raised $5.5 million.[8]

www.scripted.com

➤ **Textbroker (@Textbroker):** Textbroker is an online platform for on-demand content. Its marketplace of more than 100,000 U.S.-based freelance authors delivers articles, blog posts, product descriptions, web copy, press releases, white papers, and other types of content. Textbroker also offers custom content from professional, native-speaking authors in German (textbroker.de), French (textbroker.fr), U.K. English (textbroker.co.uk), Spanish (textbroker.es), Dutch (textbroker.nl), Italian (textbroker.it), Portuguese (textbroker.pt), and Brazilian Portuguese (textbroker.com.br). The company is partially backed by Viewpoint Capital Partners.[9]

www.textbroker.com

➤ **Zerys (@Zerys):** Zerys is a content strategy planner, content production platform, and professional writer marketplace with solutions for marketers and agencies. The Zerys content marketplace has more than 20,000 writers available for hire, more than 9,000 end users, and more than 1,100 marketing agency partners.

www.Zerys.com

■ MANAGING THE OUTSOURCED TEAM

Unfortunately, no matter how thorough the agency search, client-agency partnerships do not always go as planned. While both parties enter the relationship with the best of intentions, challenges arise and partnerships dissolve. However, many factors that contribute to relationships going bad can either be avoided or overcome, if you know the causes.

Let's take a look at agency-side and client-side factors that can lead to unproductive partnerships and the inevitable breakups.

Agency-Side Factors

Common reasons the agency may be to blame:

➤ **Financial instability:** Desperation is a very dangerous thing in business. Agencies in difficult financial positions may be forced to cut corners on staffing, take on bad accounts that distract from the good ones, and make decisions that are not in the long-term best interest of the agency or its clients. If you get the sense an agency is struggling financially, run the other way. Along those lines, ask the difficult financial questions up front to avoid problems later. Ensure that potential partners have strong cash flow, profits, and/or funding, especially when working with startup marketing firms.

➤ **Focusing on outputs, not outcomes:** Rely on agency partners that continually adapt strategies based on performance, obsess over data, and are driven to exceed ROI expectations. Avoid agencies that focus primarily on deliverables and lack systems to show how those outputs affect marketing metrics that matter to the client. Agencies that still use the billable-hour model may be the biggest culprits in this arena, by putting the emphasis on time spent rather than value gained.

➤ **Overpromising, underdelivering:** Most relationships that go bad are doomed from the start. In many cases, it is because the agency overpromises what it can achieve for a client. Expectations get set too high, and when the agency does not deliver, the client is forced to move on.

➤ **Siloed services:** Siloed activities, within your organization or your agency, create a disconnected customer experience. Strategies cannot be built in isolation if marketers want to maximize ROI. There has to be an integrated approach to a cohesive marketing strategy. Even if your business has multiple outside agency partners, their activities still must be in sync and complementary.

➤ **Stagnant business model:** According to the CMO Council, "Just 9 percent of senior marketers believe traditional ad agencies are doing a good job of evolving and extending their service capabilities in the digital age."[10] Creating compelling customer experiences, which are core to marketing success, requires a sophisticated, agile, integrated, and highly measurable approach to targeting consumers. If an agency is stuck in legacy systems and taking an obsolete approach to targeting audiences, then clients need a change of direction.

➤ **Being stretched too thin:** Financial difficulties, mismanagement, and challenges scaling to meet market demand can all contribute to agencies being stretched too thin. In all cases, it is the client that suffers. Traditional agencies are primarily driven by service revenue, so the size and capacity of the staff directly affect profits. Too many professionals, and profits quickly shrink or disappear. Too few professionals, and there is more work than they can handle. Being stretched too thin over extended periods of time negatively impacts morale, culture, productivity, and performance, which can cause clients to leave.

➤ **Talent turnover:** As discussed in the previous section, the greatest value an agency can give you is stocking your account team with top-notch, digital-savvy professionals. If the agency struggles to retain its best talent, then clients have no reason to stay.

➤ **Unbalanced portfolio:** At PR 20/20, we follow the model that no client should account for more than 20 percent of revenue. Agencies that are too heavily reliant on a select few accounts put themselves and their other clients at risk if that revenue is lost. There also is the possibility that an agency will put a disproportionate amount of energy, talent, and resources into the largest accounts, which can limit the value delivered to smaller clients. It is in the best interest of agencies and clients for the agency to have a well-balanced portfolio.

➤ **Weak processes:** Weak or no processes lead to inefficiency and lack of productivity, both of which cost you time, money, and results. Insist on a sophisticated approach to business, account, and campaign management.

Client-Side Factors

Common reasons the client may be to blame:

➤ **Conservative culture and budgets:** Great marketing agency partners can be made mediocre by conservative client cultures and budgets. If the client is not willing to adapt to changing consumer behavior and invest resources needed to improve short- and long-term performance, then both parties will end up unhappy in the relationship. Our Marketing Score research shows that the majority of organizations have aggressive growth goals and conservative budgets, creating a potential misalignment of expectations. Forty-one percent of organizations have aggressive growth goals (greater than 20 percent), but only 5 percent of organizations have aggressive marketing budgets (greater than 20 percent).[11]

➤ **Financial instability:** There is nothing more debilitating to a partnership than a financially unstable client (besides maybe a financially desperate agency). Clients in dire financial straits constantly shift expectations and priorities, lose patience with proven long-term processes, and demand more for less. Financial instability should be the number one red flag for agencies when evaluating clients.

➤ **Lack of vision:** Much like a conservative culture, a lack of vision within the client business is a nearly impassable roadblock for agencies. An agency cannot make your business or brand remarkable. Vision means that your leadership team sees opportunities where others see obstacles. An elite agency partner can play an integral role in building and realizing the vision, but it must be born from and cultivated by the client's leaders.

➤ **Low-quality product/service:** Customer experience is everything in the era of the exposed brand, and nothing will derail marketing success faster than a subpar product or service. Hiring a top-tier marketing agency will not mask or solve deficiencies in this area. Agencies should partner with companies and products they believe in. Agency account teams will struggle to maintain the necessary energy and passion when they know a client's product is low quality.

➤ **Marketing technology deficiencies:** Modern marketing success requires the right tools and infrastructure, including analytics, a sophisticated CRM system, email marketing, marketing automation, and a website CMS. If a client is not willing to invest in core marketing technologies and commit to integrating them into sales and marketing processes, then agencies will fail. There will be more on marketing technology in Chapters 6 and 7.

➤ **Personnel weaknesses:** Marketing and sales team weaknesses can be a major influencing factor on underperforming agencies, especially if the client is not willing to invest the resources needed to fill internal gaps or make difficult changes to processes and culture. Let's say, for example, that an agency is brought in primarily to build brand—website traffic, social reach, subscribers—at the top of the funnel and generate leads in the middle of the funnel. Leads are qualified through an automated lead scoring system and handed off to internal marketing and sales teams to convert. If the internal teams drop the ball through lack of effort or underperformance and continually fail to convert quality leads, bottom-line sales will give the appearance that the agency is not providing a positive ROI. Clients have to be realistic about their internal teams' capabilities, and agencies have to be able to gauge how their success will be helped or hindered by client-side personnel.

➤ **Poor management:** Weak management and leadership within the client organization commonly lead to many of the other negative factors, including financial instability, lack of vision, conservative cultures, and personnel weaknesses. There is nothing an agency can do to fix any of these.

➤ **Unrealistic expectations:** Setting realistic expectations may be the most important step in building a successful partnership. Clients have to take an honest look at their strengths and weaknesses, and agencies have to be able to assess potential and forecast success.

➤ **Weak foundation:** As we will see in Chapter 8, business and marketing core strength is critical to success. Specifically, this includes factors such as competitive advantage, corporate culture, employee retention rates, financial stability, the marketing team, pricing strategy, product/service quality, proprietary audience database size, revenue growth, social reach, and website traffic. All these factors are indicators of a client's potential and an agency's ability to accelerate success and meet ROI expectations.

The marketing industry is moving too fast to internalize everything. Businesses increasingly rely on marketing agency partners for consultation and services to differentiate their brands and drive growth and success. You can gain an advantage over the competition by taking an intelligent approach to selecting and managing your agencies.

CHAPTER HIGHLIGHTS

➤ As CMOs navigate the marketing talent gap, they are increasingly seeking performance-driven agency partners that are immersed in marketing technology and staffed with digital-savvy professionals.

➤ The future belongs to dynamic agencies with more efficient management systems, integrated services, versatile talent, value-based pricing models, a love for data, and a commitment to producing measurable results. But, these firms are in short supply.

➤ The agency landscape remains littered with traditional agencies struggling to transform their archaic business models.

➤ CMOs are turning to a large mix of agency partners and marketing service providers.

➤ Marketers still face an uphill battle in connecting agency activities to performance metrics.

➤ The right marketing agency can be a tremendous asset and play a critical role in propelling growth, but marketers must take a methodical approach to finding the right firms.

➤ Work with agency partners that care as much about performance and success as you do.

➤ The greatest value an agency can bring a client is staffing its account team with A players.

➤ Agencies whose professionals are immersed in technology trends and innovations are able to more readily adapt their own business models, continually increase productivity, evolve client campaigns, and make strategic connections to seemingly unrelated information.

➤ Prototype agencies are powered by systems that continually increase efficiencies and productivity, encourage creativity, accelerate innovation, and push professionals to realize and embrace their potential.

➤ When all else is equal, it is an agency's culture and talent that determine its ability to positively impact your business.

➤ Great marketing agency partners can be made mediocre by conservative client cultures and budgets.

➤ Customer experience is everything in an era of the exposed brand, and nothing will derail marketing success faster than a subpar product or service.

➤ If a client is not willing to invest in core marketing technologies and commit to integrating them into sales and marketing processes, then agencies will fail.

Section

III

Marketing Technology

Chapter 6—Create a Connected Customer Experience—focuses on processes and technologies, including marketing automation and intelligence engines, to personalize the customer journey.

Chapter 7—Manage the Marketing Technology Matrix—starts with the software as a service (SaaS) revolution and walks through how to navigate the ever-changing landscape of marketing technology solutions.

chapter **6**

Create a Connected Customer Experience

The customer journey is personal and in perpetual motion.

■ IT IS THEIR JOURNEY, NOT YOURS

We are living through the most transformative period in marketing history. Everything we know, believe, and practice is being disrupted. Upheaval stems from industry technology giants such as Adobe (@Adobe), IBM (@IBM), Google (@google), Oracle (@Oracle), and Salesforce.com (@salesforce), as well as emerging marketing software companies that are driving innovation.

But as fast as marketing technology is evolving, the consumer is the true change catalyst.

The customer journey is personal and in perpetual motion. The journey includes awareness, consideration, intent, decision, and validation stages, but it does not follow a linear path defined by marketers.

Social networks, word of mouth, media outlets, bloggers, brands, and books influence consumer decisions, which are researched and made while jumping from smartphones to computers to tablets. The journey can be impulsive, with consumers making spur-of-the-moment purchases through apps and mobile sites, and it can be drawn out, with dozens of resources being referenced before major purchases are made.

Every trackable consumer action creates a data point, and every data point tells a piece of the customer's story. To win consumers' hearts, minds, and wallets, marketers use technology to manage the data explosion, monitor and analyze behavior, build more intelligent strategies, and create connected customer experiences. Success requires an agile approach to campaign management, process and communication automation, integration across multiple screens and channels, and personalization through the context of consumer actions.

According to Altimeter Group (@altimetergroup), "The customer journey has evolved, yet organizations have failed to recognize and adapt to the change. Today, the new customer is empowered to make faster, smarter, more-informed decisions using technology, for instance, by accessing real-time information on their mobile devices or connecting with trusted peers across open and closed social networks. To respond to a dynamic customer journey, organizations must transform their rigid sales, marketing, and customer service programs and adopt an intrinsically more flexible organizational, technological, and go-to-market approach."[1]

■ THE IMPACT OF AUTOMATION

Marketing automation has the ability to expand the value and impact of your content, capture lead intelligence, improve lead-to-sale conversion rates, drive repeat purchasing, and, most important, enhance the overall customer experience throughout the journey.

Generally speaking, marketing automation takes traditionally manual tasks and automates them. Activities such as contact management, list segmentation, lead scoring and nurturing, A/B testing of website pages and offers, email marketing, and performance measurement and reporting can all be done more efficiently through automation.

Marketing automation is a rapidly growing, multibillion-dollar industry, but it is still in the very early stages, with relatively low adoption rates among businesses in every industry. Venture funding, mergers, and acquisitions are fueling innovation and advances in the space, opening up significant opportunities for marketers who integrate automation tools.

Some of the leading marketing automation players include Act-On (@ActOnSoftware), Eloqua (@Eloqua), HubSpot (@HubSpot), Infusionsoft (@Infusionsoft), Marketo (@Marketo), Pardot (@Pardot), SAS (@SASsoftware), and Silverpop (@silverpop). There are others, but these solutions are a good starting point when evaluating potential partners.

Automation at Work

Let's take a practical look at how marketing automation can accelerate success for your business and create a more connected and personalized customer experience.

Say your organization's primary goal is to infuse the sales pipeline with new leads, and you have a secondary goal of segmenting and prioritizing an existing lead database to identify opportunities. As in any marketing campaign, you will want to start with a well-defined strategy, determine your target audiences, establish goal values, and create compelling content assets and offers, but we are going to focus on the more technical aspects here.

Keep in mind, not all features and capabilities outlined below are available with every marketing automation solution. This is meant to give you perspective on what is possible.

➤ **Establish a scoring system.** Define what a quality lead looks like and how it behaves. Then apply an automated system to score leads as they enter and move through your funnel. For B2B marketers, important scoring criteria may include the obvious factors of job title, industry, revenue, employee size, and budget. But now that you are using advanced marketing technology, you can expand lead scoring to include actions taken, such as pages viewed, times visiting the site, webinars attended, content downloaded, social media interactions, email opens/clicks, and more.

➤ **Create landing pages.** Every offer, such as a gated content piece, needs a landing page on which to live. This is where you host the content and capture contact information through lead forms. The lead form fields sync with your CRM system, automatically populating and updating contact records.

➤ **Use smart lead forms to gradually build contact profiles.** Rather than having contact forms with 10 or more fields, use progressive profiling to improve conversion rates and gather additional information about your contacts over time. Each form submission is a chance to learn more about the contact. For example, the first time a visitor completes a form, it may ask for name, email, phone, and company. The next time that visitor completes a form, it may ask for industry and company size. Each entry is stored in the visitor's CRM contact record.

➤ **Consider A/B testing landing pages.** Not sure which image or headline to use on your landing page? Run an A/B test to show half the visitors one version and half another. You can automate this process, and then monitor results to see which version has a higher conversion rate.

➤ **Schedule social media shares across your networks.** Some marketing automation systems have social sharing built in, while others may require a third-party solution. Either way, you can schedule a variety of social updates to promote your content.

➤ **Segment and prioritize contacts in lists.** Set rules to automatically build lists based on predefined criteria. For example, you may have a "hot leads" list that includes contacts who meet a lead-scoring threshold, a "new leads" list for anyone who has completed a form for the first time, and a "power user" list for anyone who has filled out a form and visited more than 10 pages on the site.

➤ **Activate email workflows.** Once you have moved contacts into lists, you can initiate automated email marketing. As with social media features, some marketing automation platforms include automated email-marketing capabilities, while others will require third-party integration. Automated email workflows are a highly efficient and measureable way to deliver value to contacts and nurture them through the marketing funnel. Be sure to include additional resources in your emails that relate to the content your contacts have downloaded. For example, if they download an ebook, send them links to blog posts, webinars, and case studies on the same topic.

➤ **Monitor engagement.** Monitor contact interactions, which can indicate that they are progressing through the customer journey. This may include clicking on links, returning to the website, or downloading another content asset. All of these actions should be evaluated when defining your lead-scoring system.

➤ **Consider contextual content on your website.** Think about the Salesforce.com experience in which the site recommends content and products based on your past interactions. Some marketing automation solutions are bringing this technology to corporate websites through evolved CMS. By connecting your contact database to your site, these advanced systems can recognize individual visitors and dynamically alter the content and calls to action based on their history on the site. The goal is to personalize the customer experience and drive increased engagement and conversion rates.

➤ **Support the sales team.** Set up automated workflows for your internal teams. Provide them with resources and recommendations to integrate content into their sales process. You can also set up automated alerts based on the behavior of leads. For example, when a contact meets the sales qualified lead (SQL) status defined in the lead-scoring system, you can trigger an email to be sent to a specific sales representative. Or, you may set up alerts to notify your sales representatives when specific contacts return to the website.

➤ **Nurture beyond the conversion.** Do not stop at the sale. Think about the full journey, beyond the purchase, and consider what value your content can bring to customers. You can apply the same methodologies of profiling, segmenting, and nurturing to your existing customers as you do to prospective ones. For example, you can set up an automated onboarding email campaign to educate new customers, share valuable resources, and engage them in the brand.

➤ **Monitor campaign performance.** Set up automated reports to stay informed on how your campaigns are performing. Use marketing automation technology to connect activities to marketing metrics that matter and show how the campaigns directly contribute to business goals.

■ ALGORITHMS AND ARTIFICIAL INTELLIGENCE

Marketing automation gives organizations the ability to maximize the ROI of marketing campaigns and personalize the customer experience, but that is only the beginning.

In 1987, Wall Street trader Thomas Peterffy—a self-taught computer programmer—created a machine that hacked into the world's second-largest stock exchange, the NASDAQ. The computer used NASDAQ data to create and execute trades faster than humans on the exchange floor.

As detailed in *Automate This* by Christopher Steiner (@steinerwriter), an imprecise mix of past experience and gut instinct determined the actions of human traders at the time. Peterffy's machine instead used computer logic and vast amounts of data to mint money. No human on The Street could match the speed and insight the computer provided.[2]

Algorithms powered the machine. In essence, algorithms are sets of instructions coded by people and executed by computers. In practice, advanced algorithms can disrupt entire industries overnight.

What started as a hack into the NASDAQ transformed Wall Street. Today, according to the book, "60 percent of all trades are executed by computers with little or no real-time oversight from humans."

Wall Street was the first domino to fall. Now algorithms, and the coders who create and monetize them, are taking aim at new industries that are ripe for disruption.

For example, Netflix (@netflix) uses algorithms to suggest content and manufacture shows based on subscriber viewing habits and preferences. In "Netflix Recommendations: Beyond the 5 Stars (Part 1)," Xavier Amatriain (@xamat) and Justin Basilico (@JustinBasilico) share the power and value of Netflix's recommendation system. "We have adapted our personalization algorithms to this new scenario in such a way that now 75 percent of what people watch is from some sort of recommendation. We reached this point by continuously optimizing the member experience and have measured significant gains in member satisfaction whenever we improved the personalization for our members."[3]

Epagogix algorithms analyze movie scripts to predict how much money they will make at the box office and offer recommendations on how to make them more marketable and profitable, including through changes to plot lines, settings, character roles, and actors.[4]

UPS (@UPS) uses ORION (On-Road Integrated Optimization and Navigation), an algorithm-based system, to shave millions of miles off delivery routes.[5]

And Amazon's (@amazon) algorithm-driven recommendation engine may have prompted you to buy this book based on your purchase history.

Algorithms are getting smarter and infinitely more powerful, while automating cognitive tasks in ways never thought possible before. Massive transformation is on the horizon. Jobs, companies, and entire industries will be reimagined.

A 2013 University of Oxford (@UniofOxford) study authored by Carl Benedikt Frey and Michael A. Osborne— "The Future of Employment: How Susceptible Are Jobs to Computerisation?"—reports that 47 percent of total U.S. employment is at risk of computerization, which it defines as "job automation by means of computer-controlled equipment."[6] The study also cites McKinsey Global Institute (@McKinsey_MGI) estimates that suggest sophisticated algorithms could eventually be substituted for 140 million full-time knowledge workers worldwide.

Marketing is at the same zero point of algorithmic disruption that Wall Street experienced when Peterffy first turned on his machine. While Frey and Osborne report a low probability of marketers being fully computerized— on a 0-to-1 scale, marketing managers have a 0.014 probability, to be precise—marketing automation we see today is elementary when we consider the possibility of what comes next.

CAN MARKETERS BE COMPUTERIZED?

In the University of Oxford study *The Future of Employment*, authors Frey and Osborne estimate the probability of computerization for 702 detailed occupations. The report's appendix includes a table that ranks occupations from least to most computerizable.

Here is a breakdown of relevant marketing roles, along with a few other service professions to provide context. The list shows rank, occupation, and probability on a 0-to-1 scale. It does not look good for telemarketers.

0.0028 Recreational therapist (#1—*Least computerizable*)

0.013 Sales managers (#59)

0.014 Marketing managers (#61)

0.015 Public relations and fundraising managers (#67)

0.015 Chief executives (#70)

0.023 Art directors (#95)

0.035 Lawyers (#115)

0.038 Writers and authors (#123)

0.055 Editors (#140)

0.082 Graphic designers (#161)

0.18 Public relations specialists (#201)

0.54 Advertising sales agents (#312)

0.61 Market research analysts and marketing specialists (#337)

0.86 Real estate agents (#497)

0.92 Insurance sales agents (#565)

0.99 Telemarketers (#702—*Most computerizable*)

■ ORIGINS OF THE INTELLIGENCE ENGINE

Marketing automation platforms save time, improve efficiency, increase productivity, and help manage big data. They give companies unprecedented abilities to understand buyers, identify opportunities, track campaign performance, and link marketing activities to business outcomes.

But they do not provide insight into the billions of bits of data being created as consumers move from screen to screen and interact online and offline with brands.

According to IBM, 90 percent of all data in the world is less than two years old.[7] Humans are not programmed to keep up. And yet, turning data into intelligence, intelligence into strategy, and strategy into action remains largely human powered.

What inevitably comes next are marketing intelligence engines that process data and recommend actions to improve performance based on probabilities of success. Think about it. Are we really that far off from an automated marketing strategy in which the marketer's primary role is to curate and enhance algorithm-based recommendations rather than to devise them?

Humans are limited by their biases, beliefs, education, experiences, knowledge, and brainpower. All of these things contribute to our finite ability to process information, build strategies, and achieve performance potential.

Algorithms, in contrast, have an almost infinite ability to process information. They possess the power to understand natural language queries, identify patterns and anomalies, and parse massive data sets to deliver recommendations better, faster, and cheaper than people can. They already do it in health care, financial services, and customer service, and it will not be long before bots (multiple linked algorithms aimed at performing one task) descend on the marketing industry.

As Steiner says in *Automate This*, "Determining the next field to be invaded by bots is the sum of two simple functions: the potential to disrupt plus the reward for disruption."[8]

It might sound like science fiction, but for a hint of what is coming, consider IBM's Watson—a collection of algorithms and processing power capable of outsmarting the world's smartest people.

Meet Watson, Your New Machine Overlord

Watson came to fame in 2011 when it beat two human contestants on the quiz show *Jeopardy!* Among the losers was Ken Jennings, the show's longest-winning contestant. He conceded defeat in the final round by answering, "I, for one, welcome our new computer overlords."[9]

Watson used a combination of software and hardware to understand natural language questions on the show, comb massive data sets for answers, and assess those answers against even more data to determine which answer was most likely correct.

At its public debut, Watson was 90 servers in a room. Now, it is the size of a pizza box and 240 percent faster.[10]

In early 2014, IBM announced the Watson Ecosystem Program, opening up Watson as a development platform in the cloud to spur innovation and create a new generation of applications powered by Watson's cognitive computing intelligence.

Tech-savvy marketers who can harness the power of open-API algorithmic intelligence engines like Watson stand to reap massive rewards. They will be able to do more with less, run personalized campaigns of unprecedented complexity, and transform business as usual through new methods of machine-intelligent marketing. The opportunities are endless for marketers and entrepreneurs with the will and vision to transform the industry.

Imagine an algorithm-based recommendation engine for all major marketing activities and strategies. The engine will use a potent mix of historical performance data, industry and company benchmarks, real-time analytics, and subjective human inputs, layered against business and campaign goals, to recommend actions with the greatest probabilities of success. If built or acquired by marketing technology heavyweights, these tools will add algorithmic marketing strategy to the automation mix.

■ LET'S GET CONTEXTUAL

Whether you are using today's marketing automation tools or tomorrow's marketing intelligence engine, context is the key to connecting with and influencing consumers at every phase of their journeys. For example, consider how much more personalized marketing can be with answers to questions like these:

➤ What is a website visitor's relationship to your company?

➤ Where is he located?

➤ How did he find your company?

➤ What are his needs and goals?

➤ What is he looking for at this moment?

➤ What is his state of mind?

➤ Which screen is he using to interact?

➤ Is he connected to your brand's social networks?

➤ Is he an influencer in your industry?

➤ How many times has he visited your site?

➤ Has he engaged with a support representative by phone, email, or online chat?

Marketing technology is in a race to keep up with consumers and provide the context needed to create the personalized experiences they have come to expect.

Marketing in a Multiscreen World

Reaching and influencing consumers is complicated. They have been conditioned to ignore interruption-based marketing messages from brands, have short attention spans, continually shift content consumption patterns, and demonstrate complex buying behaviors. All of these challenges are magnified in the multiscreen world. As consumers move from device to device, brands are expected to adapt to needs and preferences specific to each screen.

According to Google's 2012 report "The New Multi-Screen World," 90 percent of our daily media interactions are screen-based, occurring on smartphones, PCs/laptops, tablets, or televisions. And those interactions are rarely focused on a single screen or activity. Rather, consumers are constantly shifting from screen to screen to accomplish tasks, what Google terms "sequential usage," or viewing more than one screen at the same time to accomplish related or unrelated tasks, which Google calls "simultaneous usage."[11]

The device we choose to use at a particular time is often driven by the context of where we are, what we want to accomplish, and how much time is needed. Here is a look at how Google breaks down device usage in the multiscreen world:

➤ Smartphones, which account for 38 percent of daily media interaction, keep us connected and are the most common starting place for online activities.

➤ Computers, which account for 24 percent of daily media interactions, keep us productive and informed and are most often the starting point for more complex activities, such as managing finances.

➤ Tablets, which account for 9 percent of daily media interactions, keep us entertained, are primarily used at home, and are the most common starting point for shopping and trip planning.

➤ Television's role continues to change. While it has the longest average time spent per interaction among the four screens—television is 43 minutes, PC/laptop is 39 minutes, tablet is 30 minutes, and smartphone is 17 minutes—77 percent of TV viewers use another device at the same time in a typical day. Television shows and advertisements trigger actions on other devices, but the television rarely commands the viewer's full attention.

Marketing campaigns and websites must account for mobile's impact on consumer behavior and adjust content, calls to action, and goals by device. To create a truly connected customer experience, marketers have to unify messages, functionality, and utility across all screens.

The Other Screen(s)

While market-size forecasts widely vary, all signs point to exponential growth in the wearables market, including fitness and medical bracelets, smartwatches, and eyewear.

➤ IHS Technology (@IHS) forecasts 210 million devices will be shipped annually by 2018, reaching $30 billion in revenue.[12]

➤ ABI Research (@ABIresearch) forecasts 485 million devices will be shipped annually by 2018.[13]

➤ BI Intelligence (@BIIntelligence), a subscription service from *Business Insider*, sees global annual wearable device unit shipments crossing 100 million in 2014 and reaching 300 million in 2018.[14]

Wearables are widely used for tracking activities and fitness today, but they have the potential to disrupt the smartphone industry and further the evolution of consumer behavior. Wearables present a new frontier for marketers, full of obstacles and opportunities. Soon, connecting with consumers across seven or eight screens in a single day could be the new normal.

Imagine the possibilities then.

When the Cookie Crumbles

A personalized and connected customer experience online is made possible in large part by an outdated technology. Cookies, also known as browser cookies or tracking cookies, are small text files that are stored on computers or mobile devices when a user visits a website. Every time a user returns to the same website, his browser retrieves and sends the cookie text file to the website's server.

Cookies have many different applications, including the ability to store user preferences, login details, shopping cart activity, and browsing history, which can simplify and personalize the visitor experience. Marketers can also use them to recommend content, products, and services based on past behavior and serve up targeted advertising across a network of websites.

Given the wide range of uses, websites may have dozens or even hundreds of cookies. For example, the Dow Jones Cookie Policy identifies 31 cookies that may be used on the All Things D website.[15] These include strictly necessary cookies, functionality cookies, Flash cookies, analytics cookies, advertising cookies, and social networking cookies.

Cookies are fundamental to marketing success today, but they have limitations, and their proliferation has stirred up privacy concerns.

In 2014, the Interactive Advertising Bureau (IAB) released "Privacy and Tracking in a Post-Cookie World," a white paper "addressing the limitations of the traditional cookie for providing persistent user privacy choices and tracking in an evolving multi-device, multi-environment digital landscape."[16]

According to the report, the current cookie approach to state management—which it defines as providing the information necessary for content creators and third parties to deliver personalized information and services to end consumers and respect their preferences for privacy, information transparency, and control—is fundamentally at risk for two main reasons:

1. The proliferation of cookies along with the resulting technical and privacy challenges
2. The growth and increased diversity of Internet-connected devices

The IAB report states, "The realities of the evolving digital ecosystem have resulted in the cookie being pushed beyond its useful and intended purposes. This multi-device, multi-platform, multi-environment reality has presented new challenges that the cookie is not able to address. What began as a simple state management solution has become the foundation of a complex and valuable online marketplace. This marketplace has grown to include thousands of stakeholder companies and digital consumption now extends across smartphones, tablets, TVs, and an ever-evolving array of Internet-enabled devices. In this new reality, the cookie cannot serve as the foundation for the next generation marketplace."

IAB (@iab) presents five alternative state management solutions, with guiding principles for consumers, publishers, and third parties. The report does not recommend a preferred solution but rather presents a framework for the ongoing evaluation of the cookie challenge.

The future of the cookie is unclear, but marketing technology, and our abilities as marketers to create a connected customer experience, will certainly be impacted by what comes next.

CHAPTER HIGHLIGHTS

➤ The customer journey is personal and in perpetual motion. The journey includes awareness, consideration, intent, decision, and validation stages, but it does not follow a linear path defined by marketers.

➤ Every trackable consumer action creates a data point, and every data point tells a piece of the customer's story.

➤ Marketers use technology to manage the data explosion, monitor and analyze behavior, build more intelligent strategies, and create connected customer experiences.

➤ Marketing automation has the ability to expand the value and impact of your content, capture lead intelligence, improve lead-to-sale conversion rates, drive repeat purchasing, and, most important, enhance the overall customer experience throughout the journey.

➤ In essence, algorithms are sets of instructions coded by people and executed by computers. In practice, advanced algorithms can disrupt entire industries overnight.

➤ Marketing automation we see today is elementary when we consider the possibility of what comes next. Soon, we will see marketing intelligence engines that process data and recommend actions to improve performance based on probabilities of success.

(continued)

➤ Humans are limited by their biases, beliefs, education, experiences, knowledge, and brainpower. All of these things contribute to our finite ability to process information, build strategies, and achieve performance potential.

➤ Algorithms possess the power to understand natural language queries, identify patterns and anomalies, and parse massive data sets to deliver recommendations better, faster, and cheaper than people can.

➤ Whether you are using today's marketing automation tools or tomorrow's marketing intelligence engine, context is the key to connecting with and influencing consumers at every phase of their journeys.

➤ Marketing technology is in a race to keep up with consumers and provide the context needed to create the personalized experiences consumers have come to expect.

➤ According to Google's 2012 report *"The New Multi-Screen World,"* 90 percent of our daily media interactions are screen-based, occurring on smartphones, PCs/laptops, tablets, or televisions.

➤ Marketing campaigns and websites must account for mobile's impact on consumer behavior and adjust content, calls to action, and goals by device.

➤ A personalized and connected customer experience online is made possible in large part by an outdated technology—cookies.

➤ Marketers can use cookies to recommend content, products, and services based on past behavior and serve up targeted advertising across a network of websites.

➤ According to an IAB report, the current cookie approach to state management—which it defines as providing the information necessary for content creators and third parties to deliver personalized information and services to end consumers and respect their preferences for privacy, information transparency, and control—is fundamentally at risk.

chapter **7**

Manage the Marketing Technology Matrix

Modern marketers are becoming technologists.

■ INTO THE CLOUD

In March 1999, Marc Benioff (@Benioff), Parker Harris (@parkerharris), Frank Dominguez, and Dave Moellenhoff launched Salesforce.com out of a rented, one-bedroom San Francisco apartment that Benioff called "the Laboratory." It was from this unassuming headquarters that the team set out to end traditional software business and technology models and build a global CRM solution.

According to Benioff, "I saw an opportunity to deliver business software applications in a new way. My vision was to make software easier to purchase, simpler to use, and more democratic without the complexities of installation, maintenance, and constant upgrades. Rather than selling multimillion-dollar CD-ROM software packages that took six to 18 months for companies to install and required hefty investments in hardware and networking, we would sell software as a service (SaaS) through a model known as cloud computing. Companies could pay per-user, per-month fees for the services they used, and those services would be delivered to them immediately via the Internet, in the cloud."[1]

Today, Salesforce.com (@salesforce) has become an industry heavyweight, with a market cap of more than $36 billion (as of March 2014), more than 12,000 employees, more than 100,000 customers, and an annual conference, Dreamforce (@Dreamforce), which draws more than 140,000 attendees. The company also has moved aggressively into the marketing space with major acquisitions, including Radian6 (2011), Buddy Media (2012), and ExactTarget (2013), and the launch of the ExactTarget Marketing Cloud (2012).[2]

The SaaS model that Benioff envisioned back in 1999 has become the standard for marketing technology solutions and has given rise to an ever-expanding matrix of products and platforms for marketers to navigate.

Marketing Technology Consolidation and Diversification

Venture capital funding, mergers, acquisitions, and IPOs drive a dizzying mix of consolidation and diversification in the marketing SaaS industry. For example, consider the activity over a 15-month period, from March 2012 to June 2013, involving marketing technology leaders Eloqua, ExactTarget, HubSpot, Marketo, and Pardot:

➤ **March 2012:** ExactTarget raises $161.5 million in IPO.[3]

➤ **August 2012:** Eloqua raises $92 million in IPO.[4]

➤ **October 2012:** ExactTarget buys Pardot for $95.5 million.[5]

➤ **November 2012:** HubSpot closes a $35 million mezzanine round, bringing total funding raised to more than $100 million.[6]

➤ **December 2012:** Oracle acquires Eloqua for approximately $871 million.[7]

➤ **May 2013:** Marketo raises approximately $79 million in IPO.[8]

➤ **June 2013**: Salesforce.com acquires ExactTarget in a transaction valued at approximately $2.5 billion.[9]

In the battle to own the connected customer experience and deliver closed-loop sales and marketing systems, major players such as Adobe, IBM, Oracle, and Salesforce.com are spending billions to buy complementary marketing technology companies, create app networks, and build competing cloud solutions. Meanwhile, the startup ecosystem is blossoming with innovative companies solving for niche digital marketing challenges in the areas of analytics, business intelligence, content, digital advertising, mobile, personalization, sales, and social.

So, while the industry is consolidating in some areas, including marketing automation, it continues to diversify, with new players constantly emerging, often forming new categories and subcategories that only expand the matrix.

The rapid marketing technology evolution opens up endless possibilities for marketers and brands, but it also presents enormous challenges for marketers who already struggle to keep up with the rate of change.

■ BRINKER'S MARKETING TECHNOLOGY LANDSCAPE

When Scott Brinker (@chiefmartec) first published the "Marketing Technology Landscape" visualization in August 2011, it included 100 companies.[10] In September 2012, he published the second edition, featuring 350 companies.[11] Then, in January 2014, he released the third edition, consisting of 947 marketing technology companies in 43 categories across six major classes.[12]

The introduction of classes was the key distinction in the third edition. Brinker had planned to stop publishing the graphics after the 2012 version, but then it struck him that solutions he termed "marketing middleware" were coming together to better integrate the industry. This realization led to the formation of a more meaningful and intuitive model that helped to visualize the scope of what is transpiring in the marketing technology space.

In order to understand what marketers face as they assume greater responsibility in evaluating, selecting, activating, and managing marketing technology solutions, let's break down Brinker's classes and categories.

➤ **Infrastructure:** Big data, databases, cloud, mobile app development, and web development

➤ **Internet:** Marketing environment (such as Facebook, Google, LinkedIn, and Twitter)

➤ **Marketing backbone platforms:** CRM, ecommerce, marketing automation/integrated marketing, and website/website content management/website engagement management

➤ **Marketing middleware:** APIs, cloud connectors, data management platforms/customer data platforms, tag management, and user management

➤ **Marketing experiences:** Calls and call centers, communities and reviews, content marketing, creative and design, customer experiences/voice of customer, display advertising, email marketing, events and webinars, loyalty and gamification, marketing apps, mobile marketing, personalization, sales enablement, search and social ads, SEO, social media marketing, testing and optimization, and video ads and marketing

➤ **Marketing operations:** Agile and project management, business intelligence, channel/local marketing, dashboards, digital asset management, marketing analytics, marketing data, marketing resource management, and web and mobile analytics

As complex as the landscape appears, Brinker points out that marketing backbone platforms and marketing middleware "are bringing some much needed structure to the marketing technology stack."

Platforms, such as CRM, CMS, and marketing automation, are the foundation of the marketing technology mix. These platforms are increasingly open and can be integrated with more specialized marketing software classes that Brinker terms "marketing experiences" and "marketing operations." Platforms often feature open APIs and app marketplaces in which third-party developers can release complementary products.

According to Brinker, "Middleware is the 'software glue' that makes it even easier for multiple, different products to work together. Instead of each product needing to explicitly integrate with each other product out there, middleware can serve as a common highway system for data between them."[13]

Zapier (@zapier) is a great example of middleware. Zapier lets SaaS users create integrations in minutes that push data between hundreds of web applications without having to write any code or struggle with APIs. In one instance, my agency needed to integrate our marketing automation system with our CRM system. We got a quote from a developer for $15,000 to build the custom integration. Then we discovered Zapier, and in less than five minutes we created a more robust integration than the developer was proposing, and it cost us $15 per month. That is the power of an open ecosystem.

Together, platforms and middleware give modern marketers, and their IT counterparts, a more flexible framework from which to create a connected customer experience.

■ MAP YOUR MARKETING TECHNOLOGY STRATEGY

Navigating the marketing technology matrix, which includes hundreds of solution providers across dozens of product categories, can be daunting for marketers. Features and possibilities change on a seemingly daily basis, making it nearly impossible to keep your business ahead of the curve.

Marketers used to be able to rely on IT to select and manage analytics packages, CRM systems, website platforms, and other core solutions. But now, modern marketers are becoming technologists out of necessity and are taking on direct responsibilities for the marketing technologies required to build and measure business success.

High-performing companies and marketers construct technology frameworks that can scale and adapt as new solutions and opportunities emerge and as consumers' interests, preferences, and behaviors evolve. They have a sense of urgency regarding digital transformation within their organizations, and they continually push for technologies that deliver results, specifically website visitors, subscribers, followers, leads, and sales.

Let's explore nine actions marketers can take to improve performance through marketing technology.

1. Appoint Someone to Own Marketing Technology

Businesses cannot achieve their performance potential without the right marketing technology solutions. Someone in the organization has to be responsible for the selection, activation, management, and evaluation of the partners and tools your business relies on for success.

Historically, marketers focused on the four Ps—product, price, place, and promotion—and let IT worry about technology. The problem is that IT professionals have different goals and priorities, along with larger organizational responsibilities, including data storage, security, mobility, and operations technology infrastructure. They rarely have insight into buyer personas and the customer journey, and they do not spend their time immersed in the marketing technology trends that impact your business.

Appoint a chief marketing technologist or similar leader who drives and manages the convergence of marketing and technology within the organization. For startups and SMBs, this may be your most tech-savvy marketer or an outside consultant.

2. Facilitate Continuous Collaboration between Marketing and IT

Build strong working relationships between IT and marketing teams to fully integrate and optimize technologies needed to run modern marketing campaigns. Large enterprises with chief marketing technologists are likely to have processes in place to encourage collaboration, while startups and SMBs may need new systems that facilitate knowledge sharing and better align the departments to focus on business performance goals and the customer experience.

3. Start with the Core Technologies

Assess your existing marketing technology infrastructure and identify steps to improve weaknesses. Commit to core components first, including CRM, CMS, and automation, and then build your marketing technology stack from there.

Sunset siloed products and processes. Fully integrated marketing technologies improve efficiencies, maximize productivity and ROI, create competitive advantages, and provide the critical foundation for a connected customer experience.

For organizations with legacy systems, rebuilding the core takes time. Invest the energy and resources needed to identify needs, build internal support, find the right providers, and properly migrate data.

4. Consider User Reviews

When evaluating and selecting solutions, use emerging business software review sites to see how actual users rate solutions. Here are two startups trying to help marketers make more educated technology decisions:

> ➤ **G2 Crowd (@g2crowd):** G2 Crowd, which has raised $4.3 million in Series A funding, is a user-generated business software review site aimed at making business technology as easy to buy as consumer products. Marketing product categories include call tracking, campaign management, content marketing, demand generation, digital advertising, email marketing, event management, gamification and loyalty, marketing automation, marketing resource, mobile marketing, print fulfillment, public relations, search marketing, social media management, and web analytics.[14] www.g2crowd.com

> ➤ **TrustRadius (@trustradius):** TrustRadius, which raised a $5 million Series A round in July 2013, is a professional community for sharing candid insights about enterprise technology through in-depth reviews and discussions. Product categories include all-in-one marketing platforms, blogging platforms, business intelligence/analytics, CMS, CRM, email marketing, marketing automation, project management, social media management, talent management suites, web analytics/visitor ID, and web conferencing/screen sharing. Many of the top products in each category have dozens of user reviews.[15] www.TrustRadius.com

➤ Inbound.org, a HubSpot Labs initiative created by Dharmesh Shah (@dharmesh) and Rand Fishkin (@randfish), also provides a developing platform to submit, research, and review marketing tools.

5. Become More Agile

Invest time and money to move away from legacy marketing systems in favor of more agile SaaS solutions. The SaaS revolution has democratized marketing technology. For prices starting around $1,000 per month, with little to no up-front costs, startups and SMBs can have access to the basic marketing tools—analytics, automation, CRM, CMS, email, social, and project management—needed to execute digital marketing campaigns.

Meanwhile, large enterprises that move to leading cloud solutions can more readily adapt to technology advances and maintain their competitive edges.

6. Focus Your Investments

Prioritize technologies based on business goals, and fit your technology strategy to your overall marketing strategy (more on that in Chapters 8–10). Do not try to do everything at once. If your priority goals are lead generation and conversion, then focus on the pieces necessary to build, run, and measure those campaigns.

Also keep in mind your marketing team's capabilities and capacity. Having a collection of leading marketing technology tools is great, unless you do not have the time or people to put them to use. Which leads us to the next point.

7. Put Technology to Work

Having the technology and effectively using the technology are two very different things. You can differentiate your brand and drive powerful business results through marketing technology, but only if you have an actionable plan.

Whether you build and train an internal team or outsource to tech-savvy marketing agency partners, do not let your marketing technology investments go to waste.

8. Prepare for Real-Time Marketing

Your marketing technology must take into account that consumers have all the control. They choose when and where to interact with brands, and you have to be ready in real time to listen, act, engage, deliver, and delight.

Your marketing team should be prepared and empowered to take action on a moment's notice. For many organizations, this requires a shift in approval processes and puts greater trust in and responsibility on the team.

9. Test and Revise

Always be testing new technologies, as well as new features within your existing solutions. Use free demos and trials to compare and contrast solutions, and stay in tune with changes in the marketing technology landscape. Look for opportunities to increase productivity, improve efficiency, eliminate wasted time and resources, and drive performance.

■ CORE TECHNOLOGIES SNAPSHOT

Let's take a deeper dive into core marketing technology solutions that marketers should evaluate as part of the overall marketing technology mix.

Analytics

Performance-driven marketing is not possible without data. Web and mobile analytics products give marketers the ability to gain insight into consumer behavior and build more intelligent marketing strategies.

Leading marketing automation platforms have proprietary analytics packages built into their solutions, but marketers can also gain a wealth of information from free tools, such Google Analytics (@googleanalytics) and Google Webmaster Tools. Use Google's training resources to make sure your marketing team maximizes the value of Google's products. See the Google Analytics beginner's setup guide in Chapter 8 for more details.

Call Tracking

Do you know how many incoming calls to your business result from online versus offline marketing activities? Monitoring and reporting phone call conversions is critical for many businesses, and call tracking solutions are the missing piece of the analytics puzzle.

Call tracking provides insight into who is calling, how they found you, and what marketing actions and channels drove the call.

Content Management System (CMS)

A website CMS is essential for organizations committed to building powerful, content-driven websites. There are hundreds of proprietary and open-source content management systems, so evaluate your needs and match your business goals and marketing campaign strategy to the right solution. Features to consider when selecting a CMS include:

➤ A/B testing
➤ Blogging tool
➤ File manager
➤ Forms
➤ Hosting

➤ Landing pages
➤ Mobile browser compatibility
➤ Photo galleries
➤ Product training
➤ SEO tools
➤ Security
➤ Site editor
➤ Shopping cart (if it is an ecommerce site)
➤ Technical support
➤ User permissions
➤ Version history

Note that some of these elements are standard features of leading marketing automation systems, so you will want to evaluate the CMS as part of your overall marketing technology strategy.

Customer Experience Management (CEM)

How customers engage with your brand is complex; it spans digital, mobile, chat, phone calls, social, direct, in-store, and more. A CEM solution provides marketing, sales, and service teams with insight across the complete customer journey, then goes a step beyond to help optimize that journey per the individual. This customer-centric approach is a must-have for businesses focused on digital conversions (ecommerce) and customer loyalty.

Where the CRM documents experiences, CEMs work to anticipate experiences—and to make them as positive as possible based on that individual's history, sentiment, intent, and potential. CEM platforms collect information across channels, then help businesses turn that information into actionable insight related to how to engage specific customers.

Improve the overall experience by targeting individuals with personalized video content, digital engagements (chat or video chat), promotions, or calls to action, all based on past customer preferences and their future potential. Adobe (@Adobe), IBM (@IBM), LivePerson (@LivePerson), Oracle (@Oracle), and SAS (@SASsoftware) are examples of intelligent CEM technology that marketers are now starting to incorporate into the mix.

Customer Relationship Management (CRM)

A CRM gives your marketing and sales teams the ability to manage one-to-one relationships with leads, prospects, customers, employees, partners, and other priority audiences. Use open APIs to integrate your CRM and marketing automation systems. These two solutions must work well together in order to maximize the ROI of your marketing efforts.

Email Marketing

Battle spam folders and the delete button with smarter, contextual email campaigns. Advanced email marketing solutions integrate web interactions, CRM systems, and automated campaigns triggered by events such as content downloads, website pageviews, and event registrations.

Internal Social Networks

Private, internal social business networks are valuable tools for collaboration and knowledge sharing within businesses and can be especially useful to keep marketing teams informed and in sync. Some project management and CRM systems come with built-in internal social networks. For example, Salesforce.com features Chatter. Or, you may consider a stand-alone solution to post marketing campaign performance updates and milestones, share industry links and media coverage, and keep the team updated on all relevant marketing activities.

Marketing Automation

We covered marketing automation in depth in Chapter 6, but it is worth noting its importance again here. When defining your marketing technology strategy, start with the automation solution. If you go with a leading provider, then many of the other factors outlined in this section will be bundled into your solution.

Project Management

Project management solutions help marketers manage workflows and give leaders visibility into campaigns, milestones, tasks, and activities. They can be used to share files, monitor progress, communicate without cluttering email inboxes, and prioritize actions in real time.

PROJECT MANAGEMENT SYSTEMS

There are dozens of project management systems from which to choose. If you are in the market for a solution, here are three companies to consider based on their funding momentum and popularity.

1. **Asana (@asana):** Asana was founded by Dustin Moskovitz (@moskov), a Facebook cofounder, and Justin Rosenstein, an alum of both Facebook and Google, and has raised more than $38 million. Asana's mission is to "help humanity thrive by enabling all teams to work together effortlessly." The Asana web application helps to improve the productivity of individuals and groups and to increase the potential output of every team's effort.[16] https://Asana.com

2. **Basecamp** (@37signals): In February 2014, 37Signals changed its name to be the same as its most popular product, Basecamp. More than 15 million people have used the Basecamp project management system since it launched in 2004. The product is intentionally simple and intuitive, an ideal solution for marketers who want a basic system to manage teams, projects, and workflows.[17] https://basecamp.com

3. **Podio** (@Podio): Podio was acquired by Citrix (@Citrix) in 2012. The company offers a collaborative online work platform with a built-in employee network, which can function as an internal social network, and a flexible framework that enables users to build customized project management workspaces. Users can choose from hundreds of template applications in the App Market or use the App Builder to create their own.[18] https://Podio.com

Search Engine Optimization (SEO)

As we discussed in Chapter 3, SEO today is primarily about creating content and websites that users love and are willing to share. However, there are still viable methods to gain insights into keyword searches and standard technical activities to optimize websites and local search presence. Your CMS should have built-in SEO tools, or you can evaluate complementary, stand-alone solutions.

Social Media

Social media technology enables marketers to move beyond "likes" and "followers" and demonstrate the value of social media activities. Social is an essential channel for increasing brand awareness, generating leads, nurturing prospects, connecting with peers, and engaging customers.

Leading marketing automations platforms often include social media management tools, but for marketers looking for a robust third-party solution, HootSuite (@hootsuite) is worth a test drive. The company, which has raised $189.9 million, including a massive $165 million Series B round in September 2013,[19] provides a social media management system for businesses and organizations to collaboratively execute campaigns across multiple social networks from one secure, web-based dashboard. Key social network integrations include Facebook, Twitter, LinkedIn, and Google+ pages, plus a suite of social content apps for YouTube, Flickr, Tumblr, and more.

CHAPTER HIGHLIGHTS

➤ The SaaS model that Salesforce.com founder Marc Benioff envisioned back in 1999 has become the standard for marketing technology solutions and has given rise to an ever-expanding matrix of products and platforms for marketers to navigate.

➤ In the battle to own the connected customer experience and deliver closed-loop sales and marketing systems, major players such as Adobe, IBM, Oracle, and Salesforce.com are spending billions of dollars to buy complementary marketing technology companies, create app networks, and build competing cloud solutions.

➤ The rapid marketing technology evolution opens up endless possibilities for marketers and brands, but it also presents enormous challenges for marketers who already struggle to keep up with the rate of change.

➤ Marketing backbone platforms and marketing middleware bring much-needed structure to the marketing technology stack.

➤ Marketers used to be able to rely on IT to select and manage analytics packages, CRM systems, website platforms, and other core solutions. But modern marketers are becoming technologists and are taking on direct responsibilities for the marketing technologies required to build and measure business success.

➤ High-performing companies and marketers construct technology frameworks that can scale and adapt as new solutions and opportunities emerge and as consumers' interests, preferences, and behaviors evolve.

➤ IT professionals have different goals and priorities, along with larger organizational responsibilities, including data storage, security, mobility, and operations technology infrastructure.

➤ Invest time and money to move away from legacy marketing systems in favor of more agile SaaS solutions.

➤ Prioritize technologies based on business goals, and fit your technology strategy to your overall marketing strategy.

➤ You can differentiate your brand and drive powerful business results through marketing technology, but only if you have an actionable plan.

➤ Consumers choose when and where to interact with brands, and marketers have to be ready in real time to listen, act, engage, deliver, and delight.

Section

IV

Marketing Strategy

Chapter 8—Perform a Marketing Assessment—presents the knowledge and tools to conduct a complete review of your organization's marketing potential and performance.

Chapter 9—Develop a Marketing Scorecard—demonstrates how to create a customized marketing performance measurement and reporting system for your organization.

Chapter 10—Strategize a Marketing Game Plan—features a deep dive into the principles and processes of building more personalized and agile marketing strategies using the e3 (evaluate, establish, execute) framework.

chapter **8**

Perform a Marketing Assessment

The assessment is a marketing strategy gateway.

■ POTENTIAL FOR SUCCESS

Every marketing plan should start with an honest internal marketing assessment. The assessment should consider perspectives from multiple stakeholders, including marketing and sales leaders, as well as key executives. The more involved all parties are in the entire strategic process, the easier it is to align needs, goals, expectations, and priorities.

For example, let's say a CMO, who has been in the position for only a few months, rates his marketing team above average, with perceived strengths in critical areas, including copywriting, social media, and analytics. Meanwhile, the CEO, who has more extensive experience with the team, rates them below average overall, with weaknesses across the board.

This obvious disconnect can have a profound impact on resource allocation and performance. Had the assessment taken only the CMO's view into consideration, the company may have understaffed and underperformed.

When conducting an assessment, invest the time to get a true pulse of the company's foundation, reach, expectations, and potential, all of which play essential roles in marketing talent, technology, and strategy decisions.

Foundation

The foundation tells marketers how much building needs to be done. If your foundation is weak, then resources need to be allocated to strengthen critical areas. If your foundation is strong, then time and money can be focused on short-term campaigns that produce results.

For example, let's say a company with ambitious growth goals intends to heavily invest in lead generation. Plans include adding staff, hiring an agency, and running aggressive digital paid media campaigns. Now, let's assume the company lacks a marketing automation solution, the sales team manages contacts in spreadsheets rather than the CRM system, and there are no content assets—blog posts, case studies, ebooks, research reports— to use in lead nurturing. The company may succeed in generating high lead volumes, but conversion rates and ROI are likely going to be poor until the right foundational pieces are in place.

When evaluating the foundation, primarily consider the strength of business and marketing cores, along with select performance and technology factors. Sample foundation factors that affect your ability to succeed include product/service quality, competitive advantage, revenue growth, corporate culture, employee retention rates, internal and external communications, the marketing team, marketing automation, CMS, and CRM. We further explore these factors in the coming pages.

Reach

Reach represents the size and quality of a company's network. Reach accounts for proprietary contact databases, specifically subscribers, leads, and customers, as well as website traffic volume, social connections, employees, partners, media, and other relevant audiences.

Strong reach signals a company's ability to "move the needle" at will. Companies with limited reach must rely heavily on paid media to drive leads and conversions in the short term, which increases marketing budgets and reduces ROI and profitability. Companies with expansive reach and influence can shift more resources to inbound marketing strategies that attract a steady flow of quality contacts into the marketing funnel, and then efficiently nurture them through to conversion and turn them into more profitable and loyal customers.

Reach takes tremendous time, money, and patience to build, especially in highly competitive industries. Success does not happen overnight. It is imperative that marketers set proper ROI expectations when starting with subpar reach.

Expectations

Aligning expectations for growth and success may be the most important outcome of a marketing assessment. Too often, management sets business growth goals without taking a realistic look at foundation and reach. As a result, marketers are asked to produce with inadequate budgets, talent, and technology. This is a recipe for failure.

Business success is contingent on defining priority needs and goals and aligning marketing resources and strategies to achieve them. Marketers and executives need to be on the same page when it comes to marketing metrics, priorities, and timelines.

Potential

Potential defines a company's probability of achieving short- and long-term success. Use the assessment to determine the company's vision for growth and its leaders' willingness to invest the necessary time and resources to make it reality. Financial stability, innovation, and leadership are all important indicators of a company's potential for success.

Foundation and reach weaknesses can be overcome if a company has strong potential and realistic expectations.

■ THE MARKETING SCORE MODEL

In this chapter, we cover the core elements of conducting an assessment for your business using PR 20/20's Marketing Score (@MKTScore) as a model. Marketing Score is a free online marketing assessment tool we built to rate the strength of business and marketing foundations, forecast potential, and align expectations. It is a subjective analysis from the viewpoint of internal stakeholders, including marketing management and company executives.

Visit www.TheMarketingScore.com *if you would like to complete an assessment for your business.*

After years of using online survey tools to evaluate prospects and clients, we realized that there were inherent flaws in the process and limitations to the format.

➤ It was time-intensive to turn responses into actionable intelligence.

➤ High-level consultants were required to manually analyze responses; therefore, it was not scalable.

➤ Results lacked scoring systems and visualizations that established benchmarks for performance.

➤ It failed to properly set and align expectations with success potential.

In short, a more scientific approach was needed.

Marketing Score is based on the principle that every element of an organization, as it relates to marketing, can be divided into assets, neutrals, and liabilities. Each factor in the assessment is rated on a 0-to-10 scale:

➤ Assets (8–10) are strengths that can accelerate marketing success.

➤ Neutrals (6–7) are average factors that have the potential to help or hurt marketing efforts.

➤ Liabilities (0–5) are weaknesses that require additional resources to build up and improve.

The tool includes more than 130 factors in 10 sections and takes approximately 15 to 30 minutes to complete, depending on how critically you consider each factor. By evaluating and scoring these factors, organizations can devise integrated marketing strategies; select the right marketing agency partners; allocate time, money, and talent; and adapt resources and priorities.

Section scores and overall marketing scores are represented as percentages, calculated using factor ratings. The factor ratings are combined with more than 20 profile fields, including annual revenue, revenue goals, marketing budget, employee size, industry, and sales cycle length, to gain strategic insights, establish benchmarks, and help drive change and improved performance.

How Professionals Rate Their Potential and Performance

The product was released into public beta in December 2012. Since that time, more than 1,500 marketers, executives, and entrepreneurs have used it to evaluate their organizations. In January 2014, we published the "2014 Marketing Score Report," which takes an inside look at how more than 300 engaged members (those who completed 95 percent or more of the assessment) rate their potential and performance.[1]

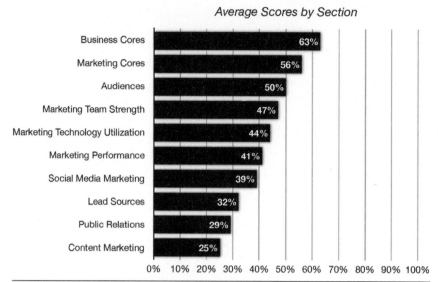

Figure 8.1   Marketing Score Averages by Section
Source: PR 20/20's 2014 Marketing Score Report.

Following is a breakdown of 15 key takeaways from the initial "Marketing Score Report." Consider how your business stacks up against these benchmark findings when performing your marketing assessment.

1. Business Cores (63 percent) and Marketing Cores (56 percent) are the highest rated of the 10 sections. Lead Sources (32 percent), Public Relations (29 percent), and Content Marketing (25 percent) are rated lowest. See Figure 8.1 for average scores from all 10 sections.

2. The vast majority of organizations indicate that generating leads (86 percent) and converting leads into sales (85 percent) are high-priority marketing goals.

3. The majority of organizations have aggressive growth goals and conservative budgets, creating a potential misalignment of expectations. Forty-one

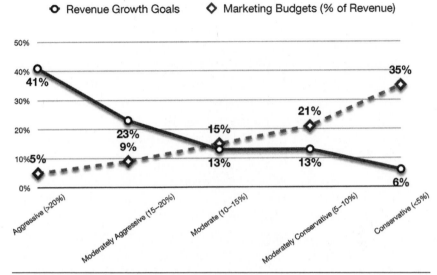

Figure 8.2   Revenue Growth Goals versus Marketing Budgets (% of Revenue)
Note: n = 318
Source: PR 20/20's 2014 Marketing Score Report.

percent of organizations have aggressive revenue growth goals (>20 percent), while only 5 percent of organizations have aggressive marketing budgets (>20 percent of revenue). See Figure 8.2.

4. Organizations founded post-1990 are at an advantage. They are more social media savvy, have higher marketing technology utilization scores, and are better at creating and distributing content.

5. KPI weaknesses at every stage of the marketing funnel affect organizations' ability to achieve business goals. On a 0-to-10 scale, here are average factor ratings for critical KPIs: customer retention rates (5.2), website traffic (4.6), social reach (4.3), customer lifetime value (3.9), lead-to-sale conversion rates (3.9), subscribers (3.8), lead volume (3.7), cost of customer acquisition (3.4), and lead quality scores (3.1).

6. Organizations lack strength and diversity in their lead sources. Key digital channels, including organic search, social media, blogging, and premium content, are all rated on average as liabilities. Sponsorships (2.0) and traditional advertising (1.1) have the lowest impact on performance out of 18 marketing channels, while referrals (5.3) and website (4.8) are the highest-rated lead sources on average.

7. Organizations lack confidence in their internal marketing teams, which are particularly weak in key digital marketing skills. With the exception of strategic planning (6.2) and website management (6.1), on average, organizations rated their internal marketing teams weak in all 15 skills that should be considered as part of a modern marketing team.

8. Many organizations lack or are underutilizing fundamental marketing technologies, including call tracking, marketing automation, and marketing analytics. A strong marketing technology foundation is critical to driving performance. Core technologies, when integrated, improve efficiencies, maximize productivity and ROI, and create competitive advantages.

9. Marketing automation high performers have significantly stronger lead-to-sale conversion rates, cost of customer acquisition (COCA), and overall marketing scores.

10. Internal social network high performers have stronger internal communications, corporate cultures, employee relationships, and employee retention rates.

11. Blogging high performers dominate all others in a number of critical marketing performance metrics, such as website traffic, lead volume, and lead quality scores, as well as overall marketing scores.

12. Revenue growth high performers have a distinct advantage in the Marketing Performance section, driven by stronger Social Media, Lead Sources, Public Relations, and Content Marketing section scores.

13. Despite lead generation and lead-to-sale conversions being the two highest-priority goals, organizations are failing to tap into the power of social media to achieve those goals. Using social media to generate leads (3.6) and to connect with and nurture leads (3.5) are two of the lowest-rated factors in the section, despite their potential to help achieve the highest-priority marketing goals.

14. Organizations are missing opportunities to generate and nurture leads due to enormous gaps in their content marketing programs. The Content Marketing section features 13 factors that can have a profound impact on an organization's success. The highest-rated factor is blogging, at a relatively weak 4.4.

15. Public relations is an underutilized strategy. Organizations are failing to use content marketing to fuel media opportunities and are struggling to maintain a strong media presence online and offline.

■ BUSINESS AND MARKETING CORES

Marketers must commit to core strength. Every organization should be focused on building assets that can be leveraged to accelerate success, including brand awareness, website traffic, social reach and influence, proprietary databases, persona-based content, industry relationships, partnerships, and goodwill. If the core is weak, then you will need to invest resources in building the foundation, adapting campaign strategies, adjusting goals and timelines, and properly aligning ROI expectations.

The following sections detail business and marketing core factors that should be evaluated during a marketing assessment.

Business Cores

Let's start with the fundamental business factors that determine if the foundation for success is in place:

Community Involvement

Does your business support employee volunteer efforts and regularly contribute time and money to the communities, events, and causes that matter to the brand, customers, and employees?

Corporate citizenship—including having a positive social impact—is on the rise, and more employees expect the opportunity to give back and engage with their communities.

Corporate Culture

As Dharmesh Shah (@dharmesh) defined in the foreword to this book, corporate culture is an organization's set of shared beliefs, values, and practices, which can ultimately determine the way employees think and act. Model cultures highly value employees and customers and encourage leadership throughout the company.

Does your corporate culture nurture positivity, performance, and innovation? Powerful corporate cultures fuel the best ideas, talent, and work.

Customer Service

Loyalty drives profitability and positive word-of-mouth. Delighted customers can be one of your organization's greatest assets—and revenue channels.

Your customer service team is often the point of most direct contact with existing or prospective customers.

Would you be happy with the experience after contacting your support? Does poor customer service keep customers from calling or drive them to switch to a competitor?

Customer service affects repeat and recurring sales, referrals, reviews, and overall customer happiness with your brand. It may not fall under your organization's marketing umbrella, but customer service strength certainly impacts your team's ability to achieve its goals.

External Communications

Do you have a sound communications strategy for all external audiences, including customers, media, partners, job candidates, and analysts? Are your communications consistent with your brand positioning across all channels? An integrated communications strategy is paramount to building brand preference and loyalty.

Financial Stability

Businesses struggling to maintain financial stability are often under pressure to keep costs down, which can directly impact the quality of products and services. Financially stable businesses are able to invest in the best people, processes, and technologies. These organizations do not act out of desperation and tend to remain committed to long-term, organic marketing strategies that lead to sustained growth and success.

Innovation

Does your organization embrace digital transformation, or is it stagnant, continually waiting for best practices to emerge and competitors to take all the risks? High-performing companies thrive on improving processes and taking risks when others are not willing or able. Highly conservative companies will always struggle to propel growth and outperform their more innovative competitors.

Internal Communications

Does your company have technologies and processes in place to facilitate collaboration and knowledge sharing among employees, reduce email clutter, and improve productivity and performance? Your employees should be your brand's biggest advocates. Strong internal communications keep employees informed and engaged in the company's success.

Market Share

What percentage of the market does your company own? Is your market share rising or falling? Are there opportunities for growth in your existing markets, or should you explore new markets for your products and services? Answers to these questions directly affect your marketing strategy and impact resource allocation.

Marketing Team

How would you rate the overall strength of your marketing team? Marketing teams must be able to envision on a strategic level, building fully integrated campaigns, and execute on the tactical level, conducting activities that drive real business results.

If your team is weak, you can invest in building an internal staff of modern marketers, or you can hire outside partners to support growth initiatives. Your company will only go as far as your talent takes it.

Pricing Strategy

Pricing strategy is critical to financial strength and has an enormous impact on marketing success. Price too high, and you may miss opportunities and fall short of revenue potential. Price too low, and you leave profits on the table and shortchange your ability to invest in the company's growth. If pricing strategy is a weakness, make getting it right a high priority.

Product/Service Quality

Would you use and recommend your company's product or service? Be honest, and think about your product versus the competition. Is it better? Does it deliver greater value to the customer? In today's always-on social-media world, product quality weaknesses can quickly undermine the best marketing strategies.

Sales Staff

If marketing delivers sales qualified leads (SQLs), can the sales team close them? The most effective modern sales professionals use technology, specifically CRM systems and marketing automation tools, to continually improve their processes and performance. Marketing can fill the funnel with leads, but sales has to convert, or your organization will continually underperform and fall short of ROI expectations.

Tolerance for Risk

Do your business leaders fear failure? Modern marketers do not wait around for competitor case studies to win executive support. Building a performance-driven organization requires a willingness to take chances and experiment with new marketing channels and campaigns.

Vision

Does your organization have a vision to achieve something great and the will to make it reality? The stronger the vision to think and act differently, the greater the opportunity for marketing to help the business achieve its growth potential.

Marketing Cores

Following are essential marketing factors that directly impact your company's strategy and performance. By no means is this an exhaustive list, but the strength of these elements is critical to the success of the organization, from both a marketing and sales perspective. They help set the foundation that drives new leads, assists in customer conversions, and encourages brand loyalty.

Brand Awareness
Do people recognize your brand name and know what you do? While awareness is a somewhat intangible asset, marketers can monitor progress through metrics such as blog subscribers, social connections, website visits, blog comments, and social media mentions.

If you are a startup, or even an established company entering a new market, your awareness is likely low. The marketing strategy will need to concentrate on top-of-the-funnel activities, including blogging, social engagement, and public relations, in order to build brand name recognition and draw in visitors.

Brand Positioning
Strong brand positioning—clearly conveying your brand story and value proposition—leads to preference and purchase. Know who you are, what you stand for, and why it matters to your audiences.

As Simon Sinek (@simonsinek) says in his brilliant TED talk—"How Great Leaders Inspire Action"—"People don't buy what you do, they buy why you do it." Start your branding with the *why*.[2]

Buyer Persona Profiles
Organizations with a deep understanding of their buyers are able to more effectively personalize the customer journey, create memorable brand experiences, and influence buying behavior. Consider pain points, needs, goals, and communication preferences when defining personas.

Competitive Advantage

What is your competitive advantage? Stop and think about it right now. Do you have a convincing answer?

If not, marketing is going to be an uphill climb. Before you invest significant time and energy in campaign strategies, develop a clear overview of the key differentiating factors that set your business apart, and then consistently convey them to your marketing and sales teams.

Customer Database

The size and quality of your customer database is one of the most critical assets in any marketing program. With a solid customer database, you can enhance marketing strategies deeper in the funnel to improve retention and loyalty—and drive revenue and profits.

Lead Database

Do your marketing and sales teams manage online and offline leads in a CRM system? Are leads segmented and nurtured based on factors such as quality scores, life cycle stage, and interactions with the company?

The quality of your lead database impacts your ability to draw qualified leads through the funnel and convert them into customers.

Opportunities for Growth

Opportunity is everywhere for unique and innovative companies that bring real value to customers. But, opportunity can be overwhelming if you do not adapt to changing markets and growing demand, focus on your core customers and capabilities, and build a scalable infrastructure.

Know your strengths and limitations. If the infrastructure is not in place, do not push growth beyond your ability to service it. If the organization lacks growth opportunities, then there may be larger issues to address in the previous business cores section.

Sales/Marketing Integration

Marketing and sales teams must be in sync to maximize lead flow, customer conversions, revenue, and profits. This requires strong communications, technology to facilitate collaboration, and a mutual commitment to achieve business goals.

Sales Process

When marketing hands off leads to sales, there must be a process in place to seamlessly transition the opportunities. Does your sales team use CRM and automation technologies to nurture opportunities, monitor leads' website visits, track communications, update contact records, and maximize conversion rates? If the sales process has holes, work with sales leaders to ensure that quality leads coming into the system do not fall through the cracks.

Website

Websites are the focal point of a connected customer experience for many brands today. Consumers are craving multimedia content on their smartphones, tablets, and PCs that helps them make educated buying decisions.

A website is much more than an online brochure. It is an opportunity to create personalized brand experiences that adapt to consumers' needs and goals in real time and drive business growth.

■ THE STRATEGY GATEWAY

Think of the assessment as a marketing strategy gateway. It forces organizations to ask important questions such as the following:

➤ Does the organization have and use core marketing technology solutions, including analytics, CMS, CRM, email marketing, marketing automation, and project management?

➤ Are technologies integrated, or are siloed solutions creating inefficiencies?

➤ How does your organization rate in key performance metrics, such as cost of customer acquisition (COCA), lead volume, lead quality scores, lead-to-sale conversion rates, social reach, subscribers, and website traffic?

➤ Is the organization generating sales opportunities from a diverse set of lead sources, including blogging, content downloads, email marketing, events, inbound phone calls, and organic search? If not, how can the marketing strategy improve the volume and quality of leads from various channels?

➤ Is the marketing team structured to excel in inbound marketing? Consider competencies in copywriting, data analysis, email marketing, lead management/nurturing, search engine optimization, strategic planning, and video production/editing. If the internal team lacks capabilities or capacity, how will you ramp up marketing efforts moving forward?

➤ How strong is the organization at creating and distributing digital content assets that meet audience needs throughout the customer journey, including blog posts, case studies, ebooks, email newsletters, infographics, landing pages, mobile apps, original research reports, podcasts, press releases, videos, webinars, and white papers?

The strengths and weaknesses identified during the assessment process enable marketers to develop preliminary strategy concepts and begin to prioritize and allocate resources.

But, before we dive into building the marketing game plan in Chapter 10, it is time to develop the marketing scorecard to monitor and manage performance.

CHAPTER HIGHLIGHTS

➤ Every marketing plan should start with an honest internal assessment from multiple stakeholders, including marketing and sales leaders, as well as key executives.

➤ An assessment provides insight into your company's foundation, reach, expectations, and potential, all of which play essential roles in marketing talent, technology, and strategy decisions.

➤ The foundation tells marketers how much building work needs to be done.

➤ Reach represents the size and quality of a company's network. Reach accounts for proprietary contact databases, specifically subscribers, leads, and customers, as well as website traffic volume, social connections, employees, partners, media, and other relevant audiences.

➤ Aligning expectations for growth and success may be the most important outcome of a marketing assessment.

➤ Potential defines a company's probability of achieving short- and long-term success.

➤ Marketing Score is based on the principle that every element of an organization, as it relates to marketing, can be divided into assets, neutrals, and liabilities.

➤ The vast majority of organizations indicate that generating leads (86 percent) and converting leads into sales (85 percent) are high-priority marketing goals.

➤ KPI weaknesses at every stage of the marketing funnel affect the ability of organizations to achieve business goals.

➤ Many organizations lack or are underutilizing fundamental marketing technologies, including call tracking, marketing automation, and marketing analytics.

➤ Marketers must commit to core strength. Every organization should be focused on building assets that can be leveraged to accelerate success.

➤ Delighted customers can be one of your organization's greatest assets—and revenue channels.

➤ An integrated communications strategy is paramount to building brand preference and loyalty.

➤ Highly conservative companies will always struggle to propel growth and outperform their more innovative competitors.

➤ Strong internal communications keep employees informed and engaged in the company's success.

➤ If pricing strategy is a weakness, make getting it right a high priority.

➤ Modern marketers do not wait around for competitor case studies to win executive support. Building a performance-driven organization requires a willingness to take chances and experiment with new marketing channels and campaigns.

(continued)

➤ Opportunity is everywhere for unique and innovative companies that bring real value to customers.

➤ Marketing and sales teams must be in sync to maximize lead flow, customer conversions, revenue, and profits.

➤ Think of the assessment as a marketing strategy gateway.

chapter 9

Develop a Marketing Scorecard

Data without analysis is simply noise.

■ METRICS THAT MATTER

Measurement matters now more than ever. Marketing executives and business leaders are drowning in data. They have access to powerful tools that produce endless streams of information about contacts, including visitors, leads, and customers. However, data without analysis is simply noise. Your company must excel at bringing structure and meaning to numbers. Be proactive in assessing performance, and be willing to adapt in real time based on results (or lack thereof).

Marketing technology advances have made it easier and more affordable to connect activities to outcomes, but marketers have largely dropped the ball when it comes to monitoring, reporting, and improving performance.

Adobe's "Digital Distress" study, which surveyed more than 1,000 marketers, found that 76 percent of marketers believe measurement is important, while only 29 percent believe they are doing it well.[1]

According to the VisionEdge Marketing (@LauraVEM), ITSMA (@ITSMA_B2B), and Forrester Research Inc. (@forrester) 2013 "Marketing Performance Management" survey, B2B marketers say just 9 percent of CEOs and 6 percent of CFOs use marketing data to help set corporate direction. The study indicates marketing dashboards that report activities rather than business outcomes are a major cause of the disconnect between marketers and the C-suite.[2]

So, while marketers have the ability to measure everything and shift resources and priorities based on performance, they often lack the tools, knowledge, processes, and executive support to take action. As the industry evolves, opportunities are emerging for savvy marketers who can effectively assess their marketing foundation, keep score of what matters, and adapt strategies based on performance.

Metrics such as cost of customer acquisition (COCA), customer lifetime value (LTV), retention rates, lead volume, and revenue growth are almost universally applicable KPIs, while supporting metrics, including content downloads, inbound links, social media reach, and subscribers, are important to show progress.

Scorecard Process

Marketing performance scorecards are simple to build and are increasingly efficient to maintain thanks to analytics platform APIs. APIs let you automatically pull data out of one source and place it into another. There are technology solutions we will touch on later in this chapter that offer robust reporting and visualizations, but for many businesses, a straightforward Excel document or Google Sheets spreadsheet with charts is a solid start.

[+] A template scorecard spreadsheet is available for download in the Marketing Performance Pack. Visit performance.PR2020.com.

The key is to align marketing KPIs with overall business goals, have a logical and well-documented process for updating and reporting results, and develop systems for turning data into intelligence and intelligence into action.

Let's walk through the process of building a scorecard using Social Business Unlimited (SBU)—a hypothetical B2B software company—as an example.

Step 1: Prioritize Marketing Goals

If you think of marketing as a funnel there are four sections—brand, leads, sales, and loyalty (see Figure 9.1). At the top of the funnel, companies look to build their brand and reach, attracting website visitors, blog subscribers, and social followers. From there, content, such as blog posts, ebooks, and webinars, can be used to move audiences through the funnel and turn qualified visitors into leads.

Figure 9.1   Marketing Funnel

Once lead contact information has been gathered, email marketing, retargeting, and social engagement strategies can provide value and a personalized experience. The goal at this stage is to convert qualified leads into sales.

Finally, at the bottom of the funnel, campaigns are conducted to increase customer loyalty, driving more sales, referrals, and profits.

These four sections represent the overarching goals to consider when building a marketing scorecard and game plan (Chapter 10). Prioritize goals based on their ability to help achieve business objectives, and dedicate the greatest time and money to support high-priority goals.

➤ **Build brand:** Strengthen brand awareness and audience reach.

➤ **Generate leads:** Create and qualify new sales leads.

➤ **Convert sales:** Turn leads into customers.

➤ **Increase loyalty:** Build a more loyal and profitable customer base.

SBU's sales team has a high close rate for leads that register for a free trial and excels at customer retention and referrals, but the company needs to drive significantly more opportunities to meet revenue goals. SBU has a growing subscriber base and social following, as well as strong website traffic, but the site lacks calls to action outside of a contact form and free trial signup. In this case, SBU places high priority on generating leads, while continuing to maintain momentum in brand, sales, and loyalty.

Step 2: Identify KPIs

Figure out the metrics that matter. What are the most important marketing metrics to your business? Get buy-in from relevant stakeholders on top KPIs, as they will be core to your strategy and performance reports.

For SBU, we know free trials drive customer conversions, but those only occur when leads are already at the intent or decision stages in their journey. So, SBU needs to identify and prioritize KPIs that capture contacts earlier in the awareness and consideration stages of their journey, and then nurture them through to the conversion. In this case, gated content downloads, webinar registrations, and product demonstrations are middle-of-the-funnel KPIs relevant to SBU.

Use the following list of standard metrics by goal type—build brand, generate leads, convert leads into sales, and increase customer loyalty—as a starting point for defining your organization's KPIs.

Build Brand

Brand metrics show strength at the top of the funnel and have a trickle-down effect to leads and conversions in the middle of the funnel. For many brands, website visits, social media reach, and subscribers are the most important brand metrics.

➤ Limited website traffic is often a strong indicator that there are weaknesses in critical KPIs throughout the entire funnel. If you are not drawing enough visitors in at the top of the funnel, then the organization will struggle to achieve lead and sales goals.

➤ Social media reach is a deceptive metric that can give a false sense of progress. More followers and likes are important, but only if they lead to engagement and action. Monitor and report social reach, but also connect social activities to referring website visits.

➤ Blog and email subscribers who have *opted in* to receive your communications are highly valuable marketing assets and priority audiences when building marketing strategies.

Here are some standard top-of-the-funnel brand KPIs that may be relevant to your business.

➤ Blog comments

➤ Bylined articles/guest posts

➤ Content downloads (ungated)

➤ Direct reach—blog subscribers, email subscribers, employees

➤ Inbound links

➤ Media placements

➤ Social reach—Facebook likes, Google+ followers, LinkedIn company page followers, Twitter followers, YouTube subscribers

➤ Speaking engagements

➤ Web—average pageviews, blog pageviews, direct traffic, email visits, mobile visits, organic visits, referral visits, social visits, time on site, visitors, visitors-to-lead rate, visitors-to-subscribers rate, visits

Generate Leads

Lead metrics primarily gauge volume, quality, and source. Assess the quantity of leads entering the funnel, and ensure that the total volume is sufficient to achieve sales goals. For example, if your sales goal is 10 new customers in a month and you have an average lead-to-sale conversion rate of 10 percent, then you would need 100 leads to achieve the goal.

Lead quality score assigns a rating to leads based on predetermined criteria, such as industry, title, pageviews, and content downloads. For your scorecard, you may report average lead quality scores each month, and then hold the marketing team accountable to driving high-quality opportunities into the funnel.

It is important at this stage to define criteria that differentiate a lead from a new contact and to establish a process to filter nonleads, such as general inquiries and spam form submissions, from scorecard reports. Otherwise, data will be skewed. Some marketing software solutions can streamline lead filtering by automating the process with rules and workflows.

You also need to determine the terminology your organization uses for leads as they progress through the funnel. For example: suspects > leads > marketing qualified leads (MQLs) > sales qualified leads (SQLs) > customers.

Here are standard lead metrics that may be relevant to your marketing scorecard:

➤ Content downloads—new contacts percentages, total

➤ Cost per lead

➤ Event registrations

➤ Lead source—advertising, direct, email, inbound calls, offline events, online chat, organic, paid search, referral, social

➤ Lead quality score average

➤ Lead-to-SQL rate

➤ MQLs

➤ SQLs

Convert Leads into Sales

Conversion metrics should focus on source and value. Marketers need insight into what campaigns and content assisted in and led to the sales conversion. This enables accurate ROI reporting and advanced real-time resource allocation based on performance.

Lead-to-sale conversion rate is a critical KPI for many companies. This metric indicates the strength and performance of lead nurturing and sales activities. Improving conversion rates is a quick way to boost growth.

COCA is another valuable KPI. COCA measures how much it costs on average to acquire a new customer. For example, your organization may target a 10:1 ratio, or $10 in revenue for every $1 invested in marketing. Keep in mind that this ratio will vary dramatically based on the strength of your foundation and reach, as defined in the marketing assessment. So, if your company has limited website visitors and social reach, a weak lead database, and minimal email subscribers, then your COCA is going to be significantly higher as you invest in future success.

The marketing scorecard highlights KPIs that tell the conversion story and provides actionable intelligence to evolve the marketing strategy. Sample conversion metrics include the following:

➤ Conversion rate—lead-to-customer, SQL-to-customer, visitor-to-customer

➤ Conversion assists by channel

➤ COCA

➤ New customers/sales

➤ Revenue won—annual recurring, monthly recurring, one-time

➤ New customer source—advertising, direct, email, inbound calls, offline events, online chat, organic, paid search, referral, social

Increase Customer Loyalty

Too often, marketers mistakenly think the bottom of the funnel is the conversion from lead to sale, when in reality, the loyalty stage of the funnel is the most important and profitable. Loyal customers produce repeat sales, recurring revenue, and trusted referrals. Customer LTV and retention rates are two important KPIs that show bottom-of-the-funnel strength.

LTV examines the forecasted value that customers bring to your organization over their lifetime. Calculating LTV is essential to determine how much you are willing to spend to acquire each new customer.

Retention rates indicate customer loyalty. If retention rates are weak, the marketing strategy should concentrate resources on engaging existing customers in order to drive revenue and profitability.

Here is a collection of standard loyalty metrics that may be relevant to your business:

➤ Active customers

➤ Churn rate

➤ LTV

➤ Customer referrals

➤ Customer reviews

➤ Engagement rate

➤ Net Promoter Score (NPS)

➤ Retention rate

➤ Revenue—annual recurring total, lost annual recurring, monthly recurring total, lost monthly recurring, month total, per customer/division/location/product

Step 3: Customize Your Funnel

Select one prime goal and up to 10 supporting metrics for each funnel section (a total of four prime goals and up to 40 supporting metrics). Your step 2 priority KPIs are a great starting point.

SBU's prime goals are visitors, new leads, new customers, and recurring revenue. See Figure 9.2 for a sample view of SBU's prime and supporting KPIs.

Step 4: Input and Analyze Data

When building the initial marketing scorecard, input a minimum of three months of historical data in order to determine preliminary benchmarks. However, 12 months

MARKETING SCORECARD

	Performance Snapshot: Prime Goals					
	Visitors	Conversion Rate	Leads	Conversion Rate	Customers	Recurring Revenue
[MONTH], [YEAR]						
Previous Month (% diff)						
Year to Date Total						
Monthly Goals						○

Goals & KPIs	Month 1	Month 2	Month 3	Month 4	Month 5	Month 6
Build Brand.						
Direct Visits						
Email Visits						
Organic Visits						
Paid Visits						
Referral Visits						
Social Visits						
Total Web Visits	0	0	0	0	0	0
Facebook Likes						
Google+ Followers						
LinkedIn Followers						
Twitter Followers						
Total Social Reach	0	0	0	0	0	0
Blog Subscribers						
Email Subscribers						
Total Subscribers	0	0	0	0	0	0
Generate Leads.						
Direct Leads						
Email Leads						
Organic Leads						
Paid Leads						
Referral Leads						
Social Leads						
Total Leads	0	0	0	0	0	0
Average Lead Quality Score						

Figure 9.2   Sample Scorecard for SBU, a Hypothetical B2B Company

of data is ideal to account for seasonal trends and to enable year-to-date and month-to-month comparisons.

Consider all the sources that provide data you can use to monitor and improve performance. Sample sources include analytics, automation, call tracking, CRM, email marketing, and social media management software.

For data sources with open APIs, it is possible to automate parts of the scorecard. For example, you can build scorecards in Google Sheets and automatically pull data from Google Analytics and marketing automation software to update scorecards. Automating scorecards will likely require developer support.

Step 5: Establish Benchmarks and Prime Goals

Once you have a representative sample of historical data in your scorecard, define benchmarks and goals. Rather than trying to set values for every marketing metric, focus on the four prime goals you defined in step 3. Assign monthly, quarterly, and annual goal values. Every marketing campaign should have a primary goal value associated with it as well. A good rule to follow is, *if you can't measure it, don't do it.*

The marketing assessment is very helpful at this stage. Goals should be realistic and achievable based on your company's talent, technology, budgets, and potential for success. Here are two common approaches for defining goal values.

➤ **Work forwards:** Calculate the average monthly percentage growth over the past six months, and use that trajectory to set monthly metric goals moving forward. Evaluate each KPI individually to account for the strengths and weaknesses of your current marketing program, and re-evaluate goals quarterly based on performance.

➤ **Work backwards:** Use sales revenue targets and work backward to the sales qualified leads, marketing qualified leads, and visitors necessary to achieve business goals. This approach requires closed-loop tracking capabilities and transparency across all functions of the marketing and sales process.

Step 6: Update and Activate the Scorecard

Monitor performance daily using your go-to tools, such as Google Analytics, and populate your scorecard spreadsheet monthly with the previous month's results. Use scorecard data to build more visually engaging monthly reports for the management team. You can create template presentations with standard charts and a consistent format in Apple's Keynote, Microsoft's PowerPoint, or Google Presentations. Be sure to include sections for prime goals' performance, KPIs by funnel section, key findings and analysis, campaign snapshots, and priority actions for the coming month.

Challenge yourself and your organization to become more metrics driven. Start with a marketing assessment to determine your current strengths and weaknesses, and then develop a marketing scorecard to monitor performance and inspire a more agile approach to marketing strategy.

■ GETTING STARTED WITH GOOGLE ANALYTICS

Google Analytics is the best free data source available to marketers. When properly set up, it provides a wealth of insight into user behavior, conversions, and campaign performance. Google offers training and certification for its Analytics product, which I highly recommend for every marketer.

In April 2014, Google rolled out Universal Analytics, which had been in beta since 2012. Universal Analytics changes the way data is collected, organized, and presented in Google Analytics. New features help marketers better understand how users interact across multiple digital touchpoints, including websites, mobile apps, web apps, and other digital devices.

At the same time, Google rolled out new terminology to unify its website and app reporting—*visitors* became *users*, and *visits* became *sessions*.

Following is a beginner's guide for marketers to use when setting up or updating a Google Analytics account. Work with a developer for the more technical aspects if you are not certified and confident in Google Analytics.

Define a Measurement Plan Based on Business Objectives and KPIs

If you completed step 1 in the previous section, you already have this covered. Know your KPIs so that you can set up Google Analytics to efficiently monitor the metrics most important to your business.

Establish Properties and Views Structure

Google uses a structure of accounts > properties > views. For example, under your company account, you may have a website property and a mobile app property. Each property has a tracking code with a unique ID. You use views to create specific perspectives of property data, and you can create multiple views for each property. For example, you may create a series of geographic-region views.

Install Filters

Filters let you limit and modify data that appear in views. You can quickly set up custom and predefined filters. For example, an IP filter lets you remove traffic from specific IP addresses. So, if you have multiple office locations and you want a view that shows only external traffic, you would simply set up IP filters that ignore traffic from those locations.

Create Account Users and Set Access at the View Level

Google Analytics gives you the option to restrict account user access to specific views. So, if you have team members that you only want to see select areas of the property, say a "Midwest traffic only" view, you can designate each user by relevant views.

Note, *users* in this step is referring to people you grant access to the Google Analytics account, not people visiting your site or app. Google uses the same term to describe both groups.

Set Goals and Goal Values

A conversion is logged each time a website or app user completes a goal in Google Analytics. There are four goal types—destination, duration, pages/screens per session, and event. Goals are set at the view level and can have monetary values assigned to them. Effective use of goals improves ROI monitoring and reporting.

Determine Attribution Report Preferences and System

According to Google, "An attribution model is the rule, or set of rules, that determines how credit for sales and conversions is assigned to touchpoints in conversion paths."[3] In other words, the attribution model shows which marketing activities and dollars produced the conversion. This information is critical for marketers to assess performance and continually adapt marketing strategy.

There are seven standard Google Analytics attribution models, as well as the ability to create a custom model. Your preferred model(s) will depend on your sales cycle, goals, and business model. Here is how Google defines the standard models:

1. The Last Interaction model attributes 100 percent of the conversion value to the last channel with which the customer interacted before buying or converting.
2. The Last Non-Direct Click model ignores direct sessions and attributes 100 percent of the conversion value to the last channel that the customer clicked through from before buying or converting.

3. The Last AdWords Click model attributes 100 percent of the conversion value to the most recent AdWords ad that the customer clicked before buying or converting.

4. The First Interaction model attributes 100 percent of the conversion value to the first channel with which the customer interacted.

5. The Linear model gives equal credit to each channel interaction on the way to conversion.

6. The Time Decay model is based on the concept of exponential decay and most heavily credits the touchpoints that occurred nearest to the time of conversion.

7. The Position Based model allows you to create a hybrid of the Last Interaction and First Interaction models. Instead of giving all the credit to either the first or last interaction, you can split the credit between them.

Visit the Google Analytics Help site—https://support .google.com/analytics—for more information on attribution models, including when each model is valuable and how to test options using Google's Model Comparison Tool.

Set Up Ecommerce Tracking (If Applicable)

If your business sells online, Google's ecommerce tracking can be applied on both web and mobile app properties. The tracking provides insight into factors such as product details, transactions, and time to purchase.

Integrate AdWords (If Applicable)

If you run AdWords campaigns, link your AdWords and Google Analytics accounts. This enables you to integrate in-depth paid search reports and track the complete customer journey, from ad click or impression through site conversion. The linked accounts give you the ability to refine and optimize AdWords campaigns.

Connect Webmaster Tools

Google Webmaster Tools complement Google Analytics data and give a behind-the-scenes look at what Google sees when it crawls your website. The information available in Webmaster Tools includes search traffic details, such as keyword queries, inbound links, HTML improvement tips to the site's user experience, crawl errors, site maps, and security issues.

Define the Events Tracking System

Events are used to track user interactions on your website or mobile app, including downloads, clicks, and video plays. You can define up to five components—category, action, label, value, and implicit count—during event tracking setup. It is important to have a clear and consistent system to simplify report viewing and analysis.

Establish the UTM Tagging Process

Any traffic that does not come directly to your website is known as referral traffic. Marketers can use UTM tagging to track and report the source, medium, and campaigns that produce referral traffic and conversions.

The source is the last place visited, such as a search engine, website, or social network, before reaching a property. The medium is the method a user followed to arrive at the property, such as an article, banner ad, directory listing, email, paid search, or social media. The campaign is the name that you associate with the program or activities that drove the session.

When defining campaigns, establish a process to ensure that the names used in Google Analytics are consistent with those used in your project management, marketing automation, and marketing planning systems.

Marketers can use Google's URL Builder tool to easily apply UTM tags and start tracking campaign performance. Some marketing automation solutions also include URL builders, which function in the same way as Google's. Each custom URL can have up to five UTM fields, but only campaign source, campaign medium, and campaign name are required.

Let's say we run an email campaign to promote this book. Here is how we may define the UTM tags:

➤ Campaign source: agency newsletter (utm_source= agency+newsletter)

➤ Campaign medium: email (utm_medium=email)

➤ Campaign name: performance blueprint promotion (utm_campaign=performance+blueprint+pro motion)

➤ Campaign content: first textlink (utm_content= first+textlink). Used to differentiate similar content or links within a single source that point to the same URL. For example, if there were two text links in the email, this UTM tag tracks the first link.

➤ Campaign term: not used. Only applicable for paid search keywords. (utm_term)

Create and Schedule Custom Reports

All Google Analytics reports are based on combinations of dimensions and metrics. Dimensions are ways of describing sessions (formerly visits), users (formerly visitors), pages, products, and events. For example, dimensions include user type, sources, and page title. Metrics are individual elements of a dimension that can be measured as a sum or a ratio.

You can create, save, and automatically email custom reports in which you specify at least one dimension and one metric. For example, let's say you want to monitor top-of-the-funnel performance in five states. You would pick the dimensions (states names) and relevant metrics (sessions, pageviews, and bounce rate), decide how to display the data, and schedule the report to be emailed to stakeholders at regular intervals.

Build Custom Dashboards

Google Analytics Dashboards pull in reports as widgets to display all your favorites on a single page. You can easily add, remove, and edit the widgets to customize your view. You can create up to 20 dashboards with up to 12 widgets in each.

Dashboards are private, unless you choose to share them. There are two sharing options: "share dashboard" and "share template link." "Share dashboard" makes the dashboard available to all other users with access to that view, while "share template link" generates a URL you can copy and send that provides only settings for the dashboard—you do not share any actual data with the template option.

Google has a crowd-sourced solutions gallery (www.google.com/analytics/gallery) that contains a collection of free template dashboards, custom reports, and segments. This is a great starting point for marketers looking to enhance their Google Analytics accounts.

■ AUTOMATE AND VISUALIZE INTELLIGENCE

Marketers must manage an ever-increasing array of disconnected data sources, including CRM, ecommerce, email marketing, event management, marketing automation, project management, sales, search marketing, social media, and website analytics. While marketing scorecards built in Excel or Google Sheets offer a basic solution to capture and report KPIs, they do not efficiently solve the challenge of bringing all relevant marketing data together into a single view or platform.

Organizations seeking more advanced marketing data management solutions likely need to consider dashboard and business intelligence platforms that provide tools to automate and visualize marketing reports. Sample providers include Chartio (@chartio), Domo (@domotalk), Geckoboard (@geckoboard), GoodData (@gooddata), Leftronic (@LeftronicCo), Qlik (@QlikView), RJMetrics (@rjmetrics), and Tableau Software (@tableau).

CHAPTER HIGHLIGHTS

➤ Marketing executives and business leaders are drowning in data. However, data without analysis is simply noise. Your company must excel at bringing structure and meaning to numbers.

➤ Opportunities are emerging for savvy marketers who can effectively assess their marketing foundation, keep score of what matters, and adapt strategies based on performance.

➤ Clearly define your KPIs and goals, have a logical and well-documented process for updating and reporting results, and develop systems for turning data into intelligence and intelligence into action.

➤ KPIs should be tied directly to business goals, and all marketing activities must be designed to achieve them.

➤ Brand metrics show strength at the top of the funnel and have a trickle-down effect to leads and conversions in the middle of the funnel.

(continued)

➤ Social media reach is a deceptive metric that can give a false sense of progress.

➤ Lead metrics primarily gauge volume, quality, and source.

➤ Lead-to-sales conversion metrics should be focused on source and value.

➤ The loyalty stage of the funnel is the most important and profitable. Consider the customer loyalty metrics that drive repeat purchasing, retention, and referrals.

➤ Goals should be realistic and achievable based on your company's talent, technology, budgets, and potential for success.

➤ Google Analytics is the best free data source available to marketers. When properly set up, it provides a wealth of insight into visitor behavior, conversions, and campaign performance.

➤ When defining campaigns, establish a process to ensure that the names used in Google Analytics are consistent with those used in your project management, marketing automation, and marketing planning systems.

➤ Marketers must manage an ever-increasing array of disconnected data sources, including CRM, ecommerce, email marketing, event management, marketing automation, project management, sales, search marketing, social media, and website analytics.

chapter 10

Strategize a Marketing Game Plan

High performers connect actions to outcomes.

■ e3 MODEL SNAPSHOT

The proliferation of marketing channels, apps, mobile devices, social networks, and content has given consumers more choices and greater control. Consumers want to be educated, enabled, and entertained, on their terms. Loyalty can be fleeting for brands that are not transparent and engaged. Companies must break through the clutter, connect with consumers, and create personalized experiences throughout the customer journey.

This chapter details a marketing game plan model designed to build core strength, spur growth through existing assets, connect actions to outcomes, and allocate resources based on performance. There are three phases—evaluate, establish, and execute (e3)—made up of 15 steps.

Evaluate

➤ **Step 1:** Complete a marketing assessment.

➤ **Step 2:** Conduct discovery research.

Establish

➤ **Step 3:** Calculate marketing budgets.

➤ **Step 4:** Build a marketing scorecard.

➤ **Step 5:** Set prime goal values.

➤ **Step 6:** Define and segment audiences.

➤ **Step 7:** Profile personas.

➤ **Step 8:** Catalog accelerators.

➤ **Step 9:** Establish milestones.

➤ **Step 10:** Construct the campaign center.

➤ **Step 11:** Develop the project center.

➤ **Step 12:** Integrate into a project management system.

➤ **Step 13:** Set up campaign tracking.

Execute

➤ **Step 14:** Launch builder and driver campaigns.

➤ **Step 15:** Adapt activities based on performance.

■ EVALUATE

The evaluate phase is used to gather intelligence into historical performance, technology infrastructure, success potential, marketing assets, competitors, industry trends, and resources. While this is a critical stage, do not fall victim to planning paralysis. High performers differentiate by doing, not planning. Do your homework, put strategies in place, and then start testing and revising.

Step 1: Complete a Marketing Assessment

Chapter 8 covered marketing assessments in depth. The assessment challenges organizations to take a realistic look at potential and performance and ensure that marketing, sales, IT, and the executive team are aligned. If you have already completed an assessment and gathered input from key internal stakeholders, then move on to step 2.

Step 2: Conduct Discovery Research

Carry out additional primary and secondary research to analyze the company, audiences, competitors, and industry. Potential discovery research elements include competitor analysis (brand positioning, marketing strategies, pricing, product mix, website), industry trends and reports, internal brand surveys, lead and customer database segmentation, management team interviews, marketing analytics reports (automation software dashboards, social, SEO, website), and website reviews (calls to action, content, design, landing pages, mobile compatibility, optimization).

Use an audit to gain further insight into marketing assessment responses, business goals, and expectations. Here are some example questions that may be asked during the audit process:

➤ What makes the company unique in the market? What is the value proposition?

➤ What are the high-priority products, services, and markets? Which present the greatest opportunities for growth?

➤ Are there plans to enhance the internal marketing team, specifically in the areas identified as weaknesses? Or will you be outsourcing select capabilities?

➤ Will the company be investing to improve marketing technology infrastructure? If so, what is the road map?

➤ Is there a set marketing budget?

While discovery research helps to formulate campaign strategies, you do not have to complete all research before moving on in the planning process. The scope of discovery work varies based on factors such as business life cycle stage, competitive advantage, growth goals, resources, and timelines.

■ ESTABLISH

The establish phase defines budgets, goals, audiences, and campaign strategies. Depending on the size and complexity of your business, this phase can be completed in as little as 30 days, or it can extend for multiple months.

Step 3: Calculate Marketing Budgets

Determine budgets early in the process so you can build realistic marketing strategies based on available resources. If your expectations exceed your internal capabilities and capacity, then this also is the ideal time to evaluate outsourcing options.

Marketing budgets are commonly calculated as a percentage of revenue, using historical or forecasted sales. Influencing factors include business life cycle stage, competition, growth goals, industry, market share, marketing technology infrastructure needs, and strength of marketing foundation and reach.

According to the "2014 Marketing Score Report," the majority of organizations have conservative or moderately conservative budgets.[1] Here is a breakdown of how organizations classify their budgets as a percentage of revenue:

➤ 35 percent = conservative budgets (< 5 percent of revenue)

➤ 21 percent = moderately conservative budgets (5–10 percent of revenue)

➤ 15 percent = moderate budgets (10–15 percent of revenue)

➤ 9 percent = moderately aggressive budgets (15–20 percent of revenue)

➤ 5 percent = aggressive budgets (> 20 percent of revenue)

When calculating marketing budgets, consider an ROI-based approach using historical performance data combined with future growth goals. For example, here is a hypothetical example that assumes cost per lead ($400), lead-to-sale conversion rate (2 percent), and revenue per customer ($100,000) stay constant.

Previous 12 Months
➤ Marketing spend = $100,000
➤ Leads generated = 250
➤ Cost per lead = $400
➤ New customer conversions = 5
➤ Lead-to-sale conversion rate = 2 percent
➤ Average revenue per customer = $100,000
➤ Total new revenue = $500,000

Next 12 Months
➤ New revenue goal = $750,000
➤ New customers needed = 7.5
➤ Leads needed = 375
➤ Budget to achieve goal = $150,000

Keep in mind that increasing budget is just one way to achieve revenue goals. The preferred alternative is to focus on strategies that expand lead volume, improve lead-to-sale conversion rates, and increase revenue per customer.

Step 4: Build a Marketing Scorecard

Compile a marketing performance scorecard featuring one prime goal and up to 10 supporting KPIs for each section of the marketing funnel—brand, leads, sales, and loyalty. Fill in the scorecard with a minimum of three months of benchmark data, but 12 months is preferred.

Refer back to Chapter 9 for more details on creating and managing marketing scorecards.

Step 5: Set Prime Goal Values

Keep goal setting simple. Concentrate on the four prime goals identified in the scorecard. These KPIs have the greatest influence on your marketing success. In the Chapter 9 SBU example, the four prime goals were visitors, new leads, new customers, and recurring revenue.

Use supporting KPIs as signals of the overall health and momentum of your marketing program. For example, seeing improvement month to month in social reach is positive, but setting arbitrary goals around the number of Twitter followers or Facebook likes is not as important to your success as visitors, leads, new customers, and recurring revenue.

SMART is a common acronym used to define goals:

➤ Specific: Clearly establishes what is to be achieved.

➤ Measurable: Quantifiable, and a strong indicator of progress.

➤ Attainable: Realistic given your foundation, reach, resources, and potential.

➤ Relevant: Connects to achievement of overall business goals.

➤ Timely: Has a target date.

Step 6: Define and Segment Audiences

Marketing technology has made it possible to personalize every campaign and interaction. It starts with well-defined and segmented target audiences. It is helpful to classify audiences by name, priority (high, medium, low), size, and type (direct, borrowed, purchased).

➤ Direct contacts are proprietary contacts who have opted in to receive information from your company. This includes leads, customers, subscribers, and social connections with whom you can directly communicate at any time. Note that some social connections are not direct contacts. For example, Facebook's algorithm determines how many of your connections see Facebook updates, so these contacts fit more in the borrowed category.

➤ Borrowed contacts are those you access through third parties, such as media outlets and marketing partners. You do not possess the list, so your ability to communicate with these contacts is controlled by a gatekeeper, but borrowed contacts can bolster your company's reach. Examples include publishing a guest article in a magazine that sends email links to its 100,000 subscribers or teaming up to copresent a webinar with a company that has expansive lead and customer databases. In both cases, your company benefits from a halo effect reach.

➤ Purchased contacts are those on email or direct mail lists that you have bought. You can communicate directly with these people, but they have not opted in to receive information from your company, and therefore they are the least valuable contacts.

Marketing campaigns should concentrate on high-priority direct and borrowed audiences first. If there are resources available after that, move on to medium- and low-priority contacts.

How effectively you develop and nurture relationships with your audiences can determine your organization's ability to build a strong brand, grow a talented team, create a powerful culture, gain exposure in priority markets, establish brand loyalty, and affect the bottom line. When defining marketing strategy, consider how the following audiences impact your company's success.

> ➤ **Analysts:** Analysts can be crucial for gaining exposure and credibility through coverage, reports, and reviews. They also are valuable sources of information on data, trends, and news impacting your business and industry.

> ➤ **Bloggers:** Bloggers can play a key role in content, search, social, and PR strategies. Marketers must account for industry bloggers with reach and clout, as well as consumer bloggers with ideas and the motivation to have them heard. Anyone with Internet access and an opinion to share can impact your brand and influence your customers.

> ➤ **Competitors:** Keep your competitors close in order to maintain a pulse on their strategies and their talent, but also to identify collaboration opportunities. In many industries, companies that once would have been fierce competitors now function more as peers in social media and are at times combining forces to advance ideas.

> ➤ **Customers:** Existing customers are your most important audience. Take a personalized approach to build relationships, nurture referrals, and increase loyalty. When defining marketing strategies, consider ways to engage customers through social media,

educate them through content marketing, and simplify their lives through digital properties, such as websites and mobile apps.

➤ **Employees:** Dedicated, loyal, and happy employees create a strong company culture and work environment and foster positive energy that can be felt by anyone who comes into contact with your company. Devise marketing strategies to keep employees informed and motivated. Give them the knowledge and tools to be a part of building your company's success, whether it be creating remarkable customer experiences, supporting social media efforts through personal networks, or referring quality job candidates to join your team.

➤ **Job candidates:** Marketing can play a valuable role in employee recruitment through brand positioning, content publishing, and social media marketing. If the organization has a goal of attracting quality candidates, create campaigns tailored to connect with and influence this audience.

➤ **Media:** Strong media relationships take time to build but can have a profound impact on your business. Maintain a database of priority media contacts, and manage communications through a CRM system that enables your team to track media interactions, interests, preferences, social activity, and coverage. Connect with priority writers, editors, and producers on social media when appropriate, position your company's spokespersons as valuable resources, and use content marketing to fuel story opportunities.

➤ **Sales prospects:** Use marketing automation tools and CRM software to nurture leads deep into the funnel and support the sales team's conversion efforts. Consider the application of content, email, social, retargeting, and website conversion optimization when constructing campaigns targeting sales prospects.

➤ **Social connections:** Social media activities should be designed to expand reach online and deepen relationships with followers and friends.

➤ **Subscribers:** For many businesses, converting website visitors into blog and/or email subscribers is a common goal at the top of the funnel. Marketing campaigns targeting subscribers should focus on delivering value, nurturing relationships, and moving them to the next logical stage in the funnel, if qualified.

➤ **Vendors/partners:** Partnerships with companies that have shared philosophies and values foster sales growth and create opportunities to collaborate on mutually beneficial campaigns. If your business does not have a large base of subscribers and followers, look for partners that do.

Step 7: Profile Personas

Develop a deep understanding of your audience personas. Personas are profiles or biographies on the people you plan to reach and influence. They are most often created for customers/buyers, but they should be defined for all priority audiences. Detailing personas makes it possible to humanize your marketing and your brand through a more personalized approach to communications. Here are sample questions to consider when building out your personas:

➤ What are their goals and aspirations?

➤ What are their problems, pains, and challenges?

➤ What is important to them in their personal and professional lives?

➤ How do they consume information?

➤ Are they active in social networks?

➤ Have they previously interacted with your company?

➤ Who or what influences their decisions?

➤ What sorts of images and information appeal to them?

➤ Do they have the desire and authority to take action?

You also want to consider factors such as geography, demographics, job title, life cycle stage, and buying cycle. Here are some actions your team can take to develop personas:

➤ Analyze lead and customer databases.

➤ Assess competitor websites and content.

➤ Check magazine editorial calendars in your industry for upcoming topics that signal areas of interest to their readers and your audiences.

➤ Conduct surveys, focus groups, and one-on-one conversations.

➤ Monitor and participate in social networks.

➤ Read industry publications, blogs, and analyst reports.

➤ Run a keyword analysis and Google Trends report for relevant topics.

➤ Talk to sales and customer service representatives.

SAMPLE BUYER PERSONA

Here is an example buyer persona, IT Ian, for a hypothetical B2B software company:

➤ **Role:** Information technology manager or director

(continued)

> **Pains:** Standardization and integration between existing systems, platform adoption, ongoing user support, security, and compliance

> **Challenges:** Data overload, incompatible systems, industry rules and regulations

> **Influencers:** Traditional and digital media, budgets, past experiences, word-of-mouth recommendations, reviews and case studies

> **Success factors:** Increased productivity, time to market, software and tool interoperability, security, and cost reduction

> **Content:** Blogs, white papers, technical implementation guides, and case studies

Step 8: Catalog Accelerators

Identify assets that can be leveraged to accelerate success and fuel marketing campaigns. Accelerators can be organized by status (opportunity, active), priority (high, medium, low), and type.

Example ways to classify the type of accelerator include audience lists (customers, influencers, leads, subscribers), content (ebooks, white papers), events, digital marketing properties (mobile apps, websites), partnerships, sponsorships, and speaking engagements.

Marketing strategies with the greatest potential ROI tap into and maximize existing assets. You can build entire campaigns around accelerators. For example, a subscriber conversion campaign could be designed to move subscribers into the lead stage. Or, you can use assets such as an ebook to add value to emails as part of a lead nurturing campaign.

Step 9: Establish Milestones

List all company and industry events that may be relevant to the planning process, such as company announcements, conferences, industry report releases, product launches, and speaking appearances. Keep track of milestone dates in a central marketing calendar for easy reference when building strategies.

The marketing team can devise milestone-specific campaigns, as may be the case with a product launch, or use them to enhance ongoing programs, such as publishing blog posts to give the company's perspective on a major industry study that was released.

Step 10: Construct the Campaign Center

A campaign is a series of projects designed to achieve a goal. Campaigns have target audiences, timelines, and budgets. There are two types of campaigns—*builders* and *drivers*.

Builders are recurring campaigns that lay the groundwork for future success. Builder campaigns, such as blogging and social engagement, are designed to create and expand assets on an ongoing basis. Drivers are campaigns that capitalize on existing assets to generate short-term returns and are often conducted over one- to three-month periods.

Think of builders as marathons and drivers as sprints. During the planning process, ensure your campaigns align with marketing goals, audiences, personas, accelerators, and marketing milestones.

The resources dedicated to each type of campaign depend primarily upon the strength of your business and marketing foundations, your short- and long-term success potential, and your marketing performance expectations. For example, a business that is weak at the top of the funnel—with limited social connections, subscribers, and website traffic—and lacking core marketing technology infrastructure may invest 80 percent or more of its budget in builders during the first 12 months.

You are going to want to manage campaigns within dedicated project management software, but I have found spreadsheets to be the best way to brainstorm and build out game plans. Let's walk through how to construct the campaign center using this approach.

[+] A template campaign center spreadsheet is available for download in the Marketing Performance Pack. Visit performance.PR2020.com.

Build the Foundation First

When mapping your game plan, start with a foundational builder campaign, which is a collection of projects designed to establish and improve your company's core strengths.

Foundation campaign projects are evaluated based on the quality and timeliness of deliverables rather than achieving specific goal values. These projects commonly fall into the categories of branding (collateral, messaging), content (brand publishing calendar, online resource center), education and training (employee social media workshops), integration (sales and marketing, marketing and IT), pricing, product development, social (profile setup), strategy, talent (internal team skills gap analysis), technology (CRM, call tracking, marketing automation), and website.

Take a Full-Funnel Approach

Once the foundation campaign is defined, take a full-funnel approach to campaign development. Consider recurring builder campaigns that will support KPIs at the top of your marketing funnel, including visitors, subscribers, and reach, and then evaluate driver campaigns designed to generate leads, sales, and loyalty.

Do not worry about resource allocation yet. This is more of a campaign wish list. When creating a campaign center worksheet, consider including the following columns. See Figure 10.1 for a sample.

➤ **Campaign name:** Create intuitive titles. Builders tend to be more general and related to the activity—Blogging, Social Engagement, Media Relations. Drivers are more specific to audience, theme/topic, product, or goal—CMO Lead Gen, September Lead Nurturing, New Product Rollout.

➤ **Property/division/product:** Use this field to distinguish where the campaign fits in an organization's structure. For example, if you are planning for multiple products, you can use this column to differentiate and sort campaigns by product.

➤ **Status:** Organize by concept or active. Active campaigns will be fully built out with projects and tasks in the next step. Concept campaigns stay in the pipeline for possible future activation.

➤ **Funnel goal type:** Classify campaigns by the area of the marketing funnel they are intended to support—brand, leads, sales, or loyalty. This helps to quickly conduct a strategy gap analysis. For example, if lead generation is the highest priority, but only one out of five active campaigns is in the lead section, then there is a misalignment of goals and resources.

➤ **Campaign manager:** Identify the team member who oversees all campaign activity and is responsible for performance.

➤ **Start/end date:** Note the campaign beginning and end dates.

➤ **Persona:** Select the specific persona(s) the campaign is targeting. Use this column to sort campaigns and confirm that resources are most heavily allocated to the high-priority persona(s).

CAMPAIGN CENTER

Campaign Name	Goal Type	Product	Status	Manager	Start Date	End Date	Persona	Primary KPI	Goal Value	Projects
Blogging	Brand	Product Z	Active	Employee 1	Recurring	Recurring	IT / CMO	Visits	5,000/month	Blog posts (4/month)
Social Engagement	Brand	Product Z	Active	Employee 2	Recurring	Recurring	IT / CMO	Visits	500/month	Social engagement, monitoring
CMO Lead Gen	Leads	Product Z	Active	Employee 1	1-Sept.	31-Oct.	CMO	Downloads	1,000	Ebook, landing page, blog post, webinar, email workflow, social media posts
IT Lead Gen	Leads	Product Z	Concept	Employee 1	1-Sept.	30-Sept.	IT	Downloads	250	Ebook, landing page, blog post, webinar, email workflow, social media posts
September Lead Engagement	Sales	Product Z	Concept	Employee 2	1-Sept.	30-Sept.	IT	Free trial registrations	150	List segmentation, lead scoring, persona-automated workflows
Customer Referrals	Loyalty	Product Z	Active	Employee 2	1-Sept.	31-Oct.	CMO	Referrals	10	Email marketing, list management

Figure 10.1   Game Plan Campaign Center Sample

➤ **Primary KPI:** Choose the singular most important metric that the campaign is designed to achieve.

➤ **Goal value:** Assign a numerical value for the primary KPI, such as number of leads or content downloads.

➤ **Projects:** Brainstorm preliminary projects that will be activated within the campaign. You will detail them, including tasks and budgets, in the project center next, but it is helpful to include rough project outlines as you move along the process. For example, a CMO Lead Gen campaign may include an ebook, landing page, blog post, three-part automated email, social media posts, and a webinar.

Here are some tips to stimulate campaign planning:

➤ Use your marketing assessment to identify campaign needs and opportunities.

➤ Reference your scorecard, and focus on campaigns that have the greatest probability of helping achieve prime goals and the supporting KPIs at each stage in the funnel.

➤ Look for activity gaps in your high-priority audience segments. For example, if you have a database of stagnant leads that sales is not actively pursuing, set up a lead-nurturing campaign to further qualify contacts.

➤ Review accelerators to confirm you are maximizing the value of top existing assets.

➤ Evaluate milestones to determine if any event-specific campaigns are needed.

➤ Analyze high-performing campaigns from the previous 12 to 24 months.

You can also use the following collection of common activities as a checklist when brainstorming game plan strategies. The list is organized by funnel goals, so focus on the highest-priority areas for your company.

Build Brand
➤ Book publishing

➤ Content (ungated)—articles, blogging, case studies, infographics, guest blogging, online resource center, photo sharing, podcasts, press releases, videos

➤ Events

➤ Mobile apps

➤ Public relations—analyst relations, community relations, media monitoring, media relations, offline networking, public speaking

➤ SEO—keyword analysis, local search, on-page optimization

➤ Social—engagement, monitoring, staff training

➤ Sponsorships

➤ Traditional advertising—billboard, print, radio, TV

➤ Web—analytics, copywriting, design, development, mobile

Generate Leads
➤ Affiliate programs

➤ Content (gated)—ebooks, email newsletters, original research/reports, webinars, white papers, workshops

➤ Digital advertising—banner ads, native ads, paid search, retargeting, social ads, sponsored content

➤ Direct mail

➤ Events

➤ Mobile apps

➤ Outbound sales

➤ Pricing strategy

➤ Product trials

➤ Public relations—analyst relations, media relations, public speaking

➤ Referral programs

➤ Social—engagement

➤ Sponsorships

➤ Web—A/B testing, analytics, calls to action, contests, contextual content, copywriting, games, interactive tools, landing pages, lead forms

Convert Leads into Sales

➤ Content (paid)—webinars, workshops

➤ Digital advertising—banner ads, paid search, retargeting, social ads

➤ Email—automated campaigns, content asset integration, copywriting, list segmentation/management

➤ Presentations and proposals

➤ Pricing promotions

➤ Product demos

➤ Reseller/channel partner programs

➤ Sales calls

➤ Social—engagement

➤ Web—analytics, contextual content, conversion optimization

Increase Customer Loyalty

➤ Content—newsletters, magazines, webinars, workshops

➤ Customer service

➤ Email—automated campaigns, list segmentation/management

➤ Digital advertising—retargeting, social ads

➤ Remarketing

➤ Rewards programs

➤ Social—engagement

➤ Web—analytics, contextual content

Step 11: Develop the Project Center

Projects are a collection of activities that make up campaigns. They have tasks, hours (or a related measure of effort to complete), and goals. Following is a list of standard fields to consider when building out a project center worksheet. See Figure 10.2 for an example.

[+] A template project center spreadsheet is available for download in the Marketing Performance Pack. Visit performance.PR2020.com.

➤ **Project name:** Give the project a descriptive title.

➤ **Campaign:** Associate it with the related campaign. This makes it simple to sort and view all projects by campaign.

➤ **Status:** Organize by concept or active.

➤ **Start/end date:** Track the project beginning and end dates.

➤ **Owner:** Pick the team member responsible for completing the project on time and on budget, and achieving the project goal.

➤ **Tasks:** Note individual tasks that make up each project. Include an estimated number of hours to complete each task to help with workflow scheduling and time management—for example, "(2 hours) Write blog post draft"; "(1 hour) Edit, upload, and publish post."

➤ **Hours:** Include total forecasted hours to complete the project based on estimates in the task column.

➤ **Details:** Include project description and notes.

PROJECT CENTER

Project Name	Campaign	Status	Start Date	End Date	Owner	Tasks	Hours	Details	Audience	Primary KPI
Ebook	CMO Lead Gen	Active	1-Sept.	31-Oct.	Employee 1	(13 hours) Draft ebook (13 hours) Design ebook	26	Ebook outlining CMO pain points and solutions	Subscribers	Downloads
Landing Page	CMO Lead Gen	Active	1-Sept.	31-Oct.	Employee 1	(1 hour) Write landing page (1 hour) Edit, upload, and publish page	2	Landing page to house ebook	Subscribers	Visits
Blog Post	CMO Lead Gen	Active	1-Sept.	31-Oct.	Employee 3	(2 hours) Draft blog post (1 hour) Edit, upload, and publish post	3	Blog post promoting ebook	Subscribers	Visits
Webinar	CMO Lead Gen	Active	1-Sept.	31-Oct.	Employee 1	(8 hours) Create webinar slide deck (2 hours) Present webinar (1 hour) Upload recording online	11	Deep dive webinar into ebook concepts	Sales Prospects	Registrants
Email Workflow	CMO Lead Gen	Active	1-Sept.	31-Oct.	Employee 3	(6 hours) Draft and upload 3 emails	6	3-part email workflow to those who download ebook, promoting webinar	Sales Prospects	Downloads
Social Media Posts	CMO Lead Gen	Active	1-Sept.	31-Oct.	Employee 3	(1 hour) Write template updates (1 hour) Schedule updates	2	Series of social posts to promote ebook	Social Connections	Visits

Figure 10.2 Game Plan Project Center Sample

➤ **Audience segments:** Define the audience segment(s) the project is targeting. For example, if you run a Q4 Customer Engagement driver campaign, it may include a series of projects targeting different customer segments.

➤ **Primary KPI:** Choose the singular most important metric that the project is designed to achieve—for example, ebook (downloads), webinar (registrations), and blog post (pageviews).

Consider the following additional fields for content marketing projects:

➤ **Publish date:** Add when the content asset goes live.

➤ **Content type:** Tag the type of content, such as article, blog post, case study, ebook, email, guest post, infographic, newsletter, podcast, report, slide deck, video, webinar, or white paper.

➤ **Topic:** Include the relevant themes or beats associated with the content. These topics are defined when building your company's content strategy and editorial calendar.

➤ **Social updates:** Draft template social updates that can be used to promote the content on relevant networks.

➤ **Media opportunities:** Tie content into the PR strategy. Identify opportunities to pitch premium content assets to media outlets and bloggers based on their editorial calendars and interest areas.

Step 12: Integrate into a Project Management System

Once your campaign and project centers are approved and ready for activation, move them into a project management system. In some cases, this may require manual entry of approved campaign activities, while other solutions offer the ability to import spreadsheets and automatically populate campaigns, projects, and tasks.

There are a number of excellent project management tools today, but there are currently limitations on fully automated marketing performance management. Specifically, project management solutions lack the native ability to pull performance data from analytics and marketing automation tools and connect results to campaigns and projects. This makes planning and management a manual and time-consuming process, filled with unnecessary redundancies across marketing technology solutions.

Marketing automation and website analytics software make it possible to track and report campaign performance but lack the context of time, costs, and human resources, which are critical to measuring ROI and evolving strategies.

Project management systems will become more intelligent and integrated over time. Marketers will have the ability to sort and filter by any campaign or project field and quickly allocate resources and develop strategies based on performance.

For example, if your team is charged with generating 500 new leads in a month, you will be able to run a query to determine which campaigns conducted during the previous 24 months produced 500 or more leads. You could then filter those campaigns by manager to find out who was responsible for the success, by hours to see which campaign took the least time to execute, and by budget to see which campaign generated the greatest ROI.

In this theoretical model, marketers will have real-time access to the information and data needed to run more advanced marketing campaigns. Here are example reports that could be run in a true marketing management system:

➤ View all active campaigns or projects.

➤ View all active projects targeting a specific audience, such as leads.

➤ View all automated emails targeting customers.

➤ View ebooks published in the previous 12 months. Sort by number of downloads.

➤ Show all completed projects that had sales as the primary KPI. Sort by percentage of goal achieved.

➤ Show all campaigns in the previous 12 months that achieved 100 percent or more of their goal target. Sort by hours to complete.

➤ Show all projects owned by employee X and completed in the previous 12 months. Sort by percent of goal achieved.

So, rather than using a list of projects and tasks that go away once they are checked off, this model introduces an agile marketing strategy and management system that enables dynamic performance-driven campaigns and resource allocation (talent, budgets, time).

For organizations interested in developing a custom solution, Podio (@Podio), a part of Citrix (@citrix), provides a flexible framework to easily build applications or choose applications from their marketplace. Podio still requires a number of workarounds and manual entry to marry performance data with activities, but it is one option to consider as the technology industry catches up with the demand for more dynamic and intelligent marketing management systems.

Step 13: Set Up Campaign Tracking

As discussed in the Google Analytics section of Chapter 9, it is important to establish a process to ensure that campaign names are consistent across analytics, project management, marketing automation, and marketing planning systems. This makes it far more efficient to track and report results.

Ideally, these platforms will be connected in the near future, as presented in step 12, thereby enabling marketers to create a campaign once and have it sync across systems. But for now, after you have defined campaigns in the game plan, make sure to create duplicate campaigns in your analytics and marketing automation systems.

■ EXECUTE

The execute phase is straightforward. Put the plans in motion and continually test and revise. Keep resources flexible to take advantage of real-time marketing opportunities and shifts in consumer behavior.

Step 14: Launch Builder and Driver Campaigns

Activate a mix of builders and drivers. Start with any foundation campaign work, such as content marketing editorial calendar, CRM optimization, database segmentation, lead scoring process, marketing and sales integration, marketing automation and analytics setup, and website redesign. Remember, foundation campaign projects are the only ones that do not have goal values. Instead, performance is evaluated largely based on quality and timeliness.

Once the foundation is in place, take a long-term approach to success with builder campaigns, such as blogging and social engagement, and use drivers to produce short-term results in leads, sales, and loyalty.

Step 15: Adapt Activities Based on Performance

Monitor analytics to deliver real-time insight and adapt activities based on performance. Use the marketing scorecard to regularly take stock of how campaigns are performing, and shift strategies and resources as needed to maximize ROI.

➤ The proliferation of marketing channels, apps, mobile devices, social networks, and content has given consumers more choices and greater control.

➤ The marketing game plan evaluate phase is used to gather intelligence into historical performance, technology infrastructure, success potential, marketing assets, competitors, industry trends, and resources.

➤ High performers differentiate by doing, not planning. Do your homework, put strategies in place, and then start testing and revising.

➤ The scope of discovery work varies based on factors such as business life cycle stage, competitive advantage, growth goals, resources, and timelines.

➤ When calculating marketing budgets, consider an ROI-based approach using historical performance data combined with future growth goals.

➤ Focus on strategies that expand lead volume, improve lead-to-sale conversion rates, and increase revenue per customer to achieve growth goals.

➤ The marketing game plan establish phase creates the performance management system, sets goals, profiles audiences, and defines campaign strategies.

➤ Personalized campaigns start with well-defined and segmented target audiences.

➤ Personas—profiles or biographies on the people you plan to reach and influence—most often are created for customers/buyers, but they should be defined for all priority audiences.

➤ Marketing strategies with the greatest potential ROI tap into and maximize existing assets.

➤ A campaign is a series of projects designed to achieve a goal. There are two types of campaigns—builders and drivers.

➤ Builders are recurring campaigns that lay the groundwork for future success. Drivers are campaigns that capitalize on existing assets to generate short-term returns and are often conducted over one- to three-month periods.

➤ When mapping your game plan, start with a foundation campaign, which is a collection of projects designed to establish and improve your business's core strengths.

➤ Foundation campaign projects are evaluated based on the quality and timeliness of deliverables rather than achieving specific goal values.

➤ Take a full-funnel approach to campaign development. Consider builder campaigns that will support KPIs at the top of your marketing funnel, including visitors, subscribers, and reach, and then evaluate driver campaigns designed to generate leads, sales, and loyalty.

➤ Projects are organized by campaign. They have tasks, hours (or a related measure of effort to complete), and goals.

➤ The marketing game plan execute phase is straightforward. Put the plans in motion and continually test and revise.

Conclusion

At its core, *The Marketing Performance Blueprint* is a story about the convergence of marketing talent, technology, and strategy, and the opportunity to build performance-driven organizations.

Success requires a commitment to evolve as marketers and as businesses. Consumers increasingly tune out traditional, interruption-based marketing. Marketers must create more personalized and compelling experiences to attract, convert, and delight customers.

Campaigns should be based on the principles of inbound marketing, which tailors activities to individuals' needs, goals, and preferences at specific stages of the customer journey. Strategies must be highly measurable and dynamic, constantly adapting to changes in consumer behavior, marketing technology capabilities, and data.

Here are 10 takeaways from the book. Use these Marketing Performance Laws to spur change within your organization, exceed ROI expectations, and outperform the competition.

1. **Align expectations and potential.** Take a realistic look at the organization's existing foundation and reach. Ensure the necessary budgets, talent,

and technologies are in place to achieve growth goals.

2. **Commit to core strength.** Invest resources in building a strong foundation, specifically high-performing marketing talent and advanced marketing technology infrastructure.

3. **Integrate at all costs.** Break through internal barriers and tear down silos. Optimal business results come from collaboration across departments, an integrated approach to marketing strategy, and a consistent customer experience across all channels.

4. **Take a full-funnel approach.** The marketing funnel consists of four overarching goals—build brand, generate leads, convert leads into sales, and increase customer loyalty. Diversify strategies and resources to fit your priorities.

5. **Balance builders and drivers.** Success requires a mix of builder and driver campaigns. The amount of resources dedicated to each type of campaign depends primarily upon the strength of your business and marketing foundations, your short- and long-term success potential, and your marketing performance expectations.

6. **Personalize the customer journey.** The customer journey includes awareness, consideration, intent, decision, and validation stages, but it does not follow a linear path defined by marketers. Connect and engage with consumers on their terms, and use tracking and automation software to create personalized experiences.

7. **Measure everything.** If you can't measure it, don't do it. Continually monitor and analyze activities to gain insight into consumer behavior and campaign performance.

8. **Embrace agility.** Adapt strategies and campaigns in real time based on analytics. Shift budget and time to strategies that produce the greatest ROI.

9. **Be remarkable and different.** Create more value, for more people, more often, so when it is time for consumers to choose a product, service, or company, they choose yours. Take chances, put your audiences' needs and goals ahead of your own, bring value to their lives, and help them find success and happiness.

10. **Move your marketing forward.** Stop making and accepting excuses. Start driving change. Build and evolve your team and technologies to become a performance-driven marketing organization and unlock your potential.

■ CORE CONCEPTS

Following is a chapter-by-chapter outline of the core concepts presented in *The Marketing Performance Blueprint*.

Chapter 1: We Have Entered the Age of Content, Context, and the Customer Experience

Audiences crave knowledge, answers, and entertainment, while marketers strive to provide remarkable brand experiences that capture the hearts and minds of their prospects and customers. Leading brands have become storytellers, seeking to engage and influence audiences in a real-time, multiscreen world, at all phases of the customer journey.

➤ The majority of professionals gain their digital marketing knowledge on the job rather than through full-time school programs. This lack of training and formal education is affecting marketers' confidence in their abilities to execute critical digital marketing functions.

➤ Marketers are being called upon to take leading roles in the selection, activation, and management of marketing technology solutions.

➤ Marketers must go beyond storytelling to deliver personalized, highly relevant communications across all channels.

➤ Gaps in marketing talent, technology, and strategy are leading to the most significant gap of all—the performance gap.

Chapter 2: There Has Never Been a Better Time to Be a Marketer

The future of your business and your marketing career depend on your ability to meet increasing ROI demands and continually adapt to new marketing tools, philosophies, and channels. Marketers are drowning in data, dealing with the complexities of real-time marketing, and navigating brands through the openness and transparency inherent to social media. But marketing can be more intelligent, measureable, and powerful. It can be an asset, not an expense.

➤ Marketers must develop strong analytics knowledge and capabilities in order to continually prove the value of marketing to CEOs, CFOs, and the rest of the executive team.

➤ Differentiation and competitive advantage come from taking chances. Modern marketers are continually testing new marketing technologies and strategies.

➤ Marketing must break down its own silos (advertising, communications, content, digital, PR, SEO, social, web) and find innovative ways to collaborate with sales, finance, IT, customer service, and HR.

➤ Professionals and businesses that are nimble, dynamic, and transparent have the opportunity to disrupt markets, displace leaders, and redefine industries.

Chapter 3: The Battle for Top Talent Is Brewing

A marketing talent war has begun for tech-savvy, hybrid marketers who are capable of building, managing, and executing fully integrated campaigns that produce measurable results. These prototype marketers are able to deliver services across multiple marketing disciplines, including analytics, content, email, mobile, search, social, PR, and web. They are agile, adept at advanced marketing technologies, and experts at inbound strategy.

➤ Content creation, and the ability to write persuasive copy for all marketing channels, is possibly the most important fundamental modern-marketing skill.

➤ Marketers must have strong analytical skills, specifically the ability to interpret website and marketing data, gauge campaign performance, and clearly communicate results to executives.

➤ Businesses must compete for the limited number of qualified digital-savvy inbound marketing professionals while building strategies to discover and nurture candidates with A-player potential from diverse educational backgrounds.

➤ To attract top talent, think like modern marketers and put inbound marketing strategy and technology to work.

Chapter 4: Businesses Must Take the Initiative to Mold Their Own Modern Marketers

As demand for performance-driven, digital-savvy talent rises, universities are struggling to prepare students for the reality of a rapidly changing industry. High-performing companies find candidates at all levels with the necessary core competencies and traits (strong writing abilities, detail-oriented, analytical, strategic, curious, intrinsically motivated), train them through a blend of internal and external resources, and immerse them in marketing technology and strategy.

➤ While higher education as a whole is behind the digital marketing transformation curve, there are outliers making tremendous efforts to advance their students.

➤ Businesses can tap into the wealth of content and experts available online to build their own internal academies.

➤ The opportunity exists for businesses, large and small, to create a competitive advantage through talent.

➤ Standard internal academy education paths lay the framework, but personalized advancement plans optimize the learning experience.

Chapter 5: The Marketing Industry Is Moving Too Fast to Internalize Everything

The marketing services industry is in a state of flux. As CMOs navigate the marketing talent gap, they are increasingly seeking performance-driven agency partners who are immersed in marketing technology and staffed with digital-savvy professionals. The right marketing agency can be a tremendous asset to your organization and play a critical role in propelling growth, but marketers must take a methodical approach to finding the right firms.

➤ The future belongs to dynamic agencies with more efficient management systems, integrated services, versatile talent, value-based pricing models, a love for data, and a commitment to producing measurable results. But these firms are in short supply.

➤ The greatest value an agency can bring a client is staffing its account team with A players.

➤ Agencies whose professionals are immersed in technology trends and innovations are able to more readily adapt their own business models, continually increase productivity, evolve client campaigns, and make strategic connections to seemingly unrelated information.

➤ When all else is equal, it is an agency's culture and talent that determine its ability to positively impact your business.

Chapter 6: The Customer Journey Is Personal and in Perpetual Motion

As fast as marketing technology is evolving, the consumer is the true change catalyst. Social networks, word of mouth, media outlets, bloggers, brands, and books influence consumer decisions, which are researched and made while jumping from smartphones to computers to tablets. The journey can be impulsive, with consumers making spur-of-the-moment purchases through apps and mobile sites, and it can be drawn out, with dozens of resources being referenced before major purchases are made.

➤ Every trackable consumer action creates a data point, and every data point tells a piece of the customer's story.

➤ Marketers use technology to manage the data explosion, monitor and analyze behavior, build more intelligent strategies, and create connected customer experiences.

➤ Marketing automation we see today is elementary when we consider the possibility of what comes next.

➤ Marketing technology is in a race to keep up with consumers and provide the context needed to create the personalized experiences consumers have come to expect.

Chapter 7: Modern Marketers Are Becoming Technologists

The rapid marketing technology evolution opens up endless possibilities for marketers and brands, but it also presents enormous challenges for marketers who already struggle to keep up with the rate of change.

➤ The SaaS model that Salesforce.com founder Marc Benioff envisioned back in 1999 has become the standard for marketing technology solutions and has given rise to an ever-expanding matrix of products and platforms for marketers to navigate.

➤ Marketers used to be able to rely on IT to select and manage analytics packages, CRM systems, website platforms, and other core solutions. But modern marketers are taking on direct responsibilities for the marketing technologies required to build and measure business success.

➤ Prioritize technologies based on business goals, and fit your technology strategy to your overall marketing strategy.

➤ You can differentiate your brand and drive powerful business results through marketing technology, but only if you have an actionable plan.

Chapter 8: The Assessment Is a Marketing Strategy Gateway

Every marketing plan should start with an honest internal marketing assessment. The assessment should consider perspectives from multiple stakeholders, including marketing and sales leaders, as well as key executives. The strengths and weaknesses identified during the assessment process enable marketers to develop preliminary strategy concepts and begin to prioritize and allocate resources.

➤ An assessment provides insight into your company's foundation, reach, expectations, and potential, all of which play essential roles in marketing talent, technology, and strategy decisions.

➤ Aligning expectations for growth and success may be the most important outcome of a marketing assessment.

➤ KPI weaknesses at every stage of the marketing funnel affect the ability of organizations to achieve business goals.

➤ Every organization should be focused on building assets that can be leveraged to accelerate success.

Chapter 9: Data without Analysis Is Simply Noise

Marketing executives and business leaders are drowning in data. They have access to powerful tools that produce endless streams of information about contacts, including visitors, leads, and customers. Your company must excel at bringing structure and meaning to numbers. Be proactive in assessing performance, and be willing to adapt in real time based on results (or lack thereof).

➤ Opportunities are emerging for savvy marketers who can effectively assess their marketing foundation, keep score of what matters, and adapt strategies based on performance.

➤ Clearly define your KPIs and goals, have a logical and well-documented process for updating and reporting results, and develop systems for turning data into intelligence and intelligence into action.

➤ KPIs should be tied directly to business goals, and all marketing activities must be designed to achieve them.

➤ Goals should be realistic and achievable based on your company's talent, technology, budgets, and potential for success.

Chapter 10: High Performers Connect Actions to Outcomes

The proliferation of marketing channels, apps, mobile devices, social networks, and content has given consumers more choices and greater control. Consumers want to be educated, enabled, and entertained, on their terms. Loyalty can be fleeting for brands that are not transparent and engaged. Companies must break through the clutter, connect with consumers, and create personalized experiences throughout the customer journey.

➤ High performers differentiate by doing, not planning. Do your homework, put strategies in place, and then start testing and revising.

➤ When calculating marketing budgets, consider an ROI-based approach using historical performance data, combined with future growth goals.

➤ Marketing strategies with the greatest potential ROI tap into and maximize existing assets.

➤ Take a full-funnel approach to campaign development. Consider builder campaigns that will support

KPIs at the top of your marketing funnel, including visitors, subscribers, and reach, and then evaluate driver campaigns designed to generate leads, sales, and loyalty.

Thank You

Thank you for reading *The Marketing Performance Blueprint*. I hope the book plays a small role in helping you unlock your potential as a marketer and accelerate success for your organization. Visit performance.PR2020.com to download the Marketing Performance Pack, which includes a collection of template spreadsheets referenced throughout the book.

I would love to hear from you if you have comments or questions about the book. Connect with me on Twitter (@PaulRoetzer), use the #MKTBlueprint hashtag, or email me at booknotes@pr2020.com.

Resources

Visit performance.PR2020.com

Go to performance.PR2020.com to download the Marketing Performance Pack referenced throughout the book. This free resource features a collection of template spreadsheets, including a marketing team skills assessment, scorecard, campaign center, and project center.

The site also includes case studies, tools, reports, ebooks, and other supporting materials designed to help advance your career and business.

Complete a Marketing Score Assessment

Chapter 8 features Marketing Score, a free online assessment tool built to rate the strength of business and marketing foundations, forecast potential, and align expectations. It is a subjective analysis from the viewpoint of internal stakeholders, including marketing management and company executives.

The tool includes more than 130 factors in 10 sections and takes approximately 15 to 30 minutes to complete, depending on how critically you consider each factor. By evaluating and scoring these factors, organizations can devise integrated marketing strategies; select the right marketing agency partners; allocate time, money, and talent; and adapt resources and priorities.

The Marketing Score website—www.TheMarketing Score.com—also includes a resources section featuring recommended blogs, books, industry events, and influencers.

Connect

- ➤ Twitter: @PaulRoetzer
- ➤ Book hashtag: #MKTBlueprint
- ➤ Email: booknotes@pr2020.com
- ➤ LinkedIn: www.linkedin.com/in/paulroetzer/

Notes

■ INTRODUCTION

1. "Digital Distress: What Keeps Marketers Up at Night?," Adobe Systems Incorporated, September 23, 2013, http://blogs.adobe.com/conversations/2013/09/digital-distress-what-keeps-marketers-up-at-night.html.

■ CHAPTER 1: MIND THE GAPS

1. "The Marketing Skills Gap is Very Real," Eloqua, April 17, 2012, http://blog.eloqua.com/marketing-skills-gap/.
2. "B2B CMOs Must Evolve or Move On," Forrester, July 11, 2013, www.forrester.com/B2B + CMOs + Must + Evolve + Or + Move + On/fulltext/-/E-RES96881.
3. Brian Whipple and Baiju Shah, "Turbulence for the CMO: Charting a Path for the Seamless Customer Experience," Accenture, April 22, 2013, www.accenture.com/us-en/Pages/insight-turbulence-cmo-summary.aspx.
4. Scott Brinker, "50% of All New Marketing Hires Will Be Technical," Chief Marketing Technologist blog, January 13, 2013, http://chiefmartec.com/2013/01/50-of-all-new-marketing-hires-will-be-technical/.
5. Laura McLellan, "By 2017 the CMO Will Spend More on IT Than the CIO," Gartner Inc., January 3, 2013, http://my.gartner.com/portal/server.pt?open=512&objID=202&mode=2&PageID=5553&ref=webinar-rss&resId=1871515.
6. Michael Fitzgerald, Nina Kruschwitz, Didier Bonnet, and Michael Welch, "Embracing Digital Technology: A New Strategic Imperative," *MIT Sloan Management Review* and Capgemini Consulting, October 8, 2013, http://sloanreview.mit.edu/projects/embracing-digital-technology.
7. "The 2014 Marketing Score Report: An Inside Look at How Professionals Rate Their Marketing Potential and Performance," PR 20/20,

December 10, 2013, www.themarketingscore.com/blog/bid/358790/The-2014-Marketing-Score-Report-An-Inside-Look-at-How-Professionals-Rate-Their-Marketing-Potential-and-Performance.

8. "Digital Distress: What Keeps Marketers Up at Night?," Adobe Systems Incorporated, September 23, 2013, http://blogs.adobe.com/conversations/2013/09/digital-distress-what-keeps-marketers-up-at-night.html.

9. "Zero Moment of Truth (ZMOT)," Google, accessed March 19, 2014, www.thinkwithgoogle.com/collections/zero-moment-truth.html.

10. Lori Wizdo, "Buyer Behavior Helps B2B Marketers Guide the Buyer's Journey," Forrester, October 4, 2012, http://blogs.forrester.com/lori_wizdo/12-10-04-buyer_behavior_helps_b2b_marketers_guide_the_buyers_journey.

11. Jay Baer, *Youtility: Why Smart Marketing Is About Help Not Hype* (New York: Penguin Group, 2013).

12. "The 2014 Marketing Score Report."

13. Whipple and Shah, "Turbulence for the CMO."

■ CHAPTER 2: COMMIT TO DIGITAL TRANSFORMATION

1. "The CMO Survey," CMO Survey, last modified February 2014, www.cmosurvey.org/results/.

2. Michael Fitzgerald, Nina Kruschwitz, Didier Bonnet, and Michael Welch, "Embracing Digital Technology: A New Strategic Imperative," *MIT Sloan Management Review* and Capgemini Consulting, October 8, 2013, http://sloanreview.mit.edu/projects/embracing-digital-technology.

3. Paul Roetzer, *The Marketing Agency Blueprint: The Handbook for Building Hybrid PR, SEO, Content, Advertising, and Web Firms* (Hoboken, NJ: John Wiley & Sons, 2012).

4. Scott Brinker, "Marketing Technology Landscape Supergraphic (2014)," Chief Marketing Technologist blog, January 7, 2014, http://chiefmartec.com/2014/01/marketing-technology-landscape-supergraphic-2014/.

■ CHAPTER 3: BUILD A MODERN MARKETING TEAM

1. Anita Newton, "Overcoming Extinction: 5 Tips to Stay Ahead of the Ever-Changing Marketing Curve," Adknowledge, January 10, 2014, www.adknowledge.com/blog/stay-ahead-marketing-curve-tips/.

2. Anita Newton, vice president of corporate marketing at Adknowledge, marketing talent interview by Paul Roetzer (March 3, 2014 via email).

3. Brian Whipple and Baiju Shah, "Turbulence for the CMO: Charting a Path for the Seamless Customer Experience," Accenture, April 22, 2013, http://www.accenture.com/us-en/Pages/insight-turbulence-cmo-summary.aspx.

4. Eric Wittlake, "7 Characteristics of Tomorrow's Best B2B Marketers," B2B Digital Marketing, August 28, 2012, http://b2bdigital.net/2012/08/28/best-b2b-marketers/.

5. "From Stretched to Strengthened: Insights from the Global Chief Marketing Officer Study," IBM Corporation, October 2011, www-01.ibm.com/common/ssi/cgi-bin/ssialias?infotype=PM&subtype=XB&htmlfid=GBE03433USEN.

6. Anna Bird and Patrick Spenner, "Marketers Flunk the Big Data Test," Harvard Business Review, August 16, 2012, http://blogs.hbr.org/2012/08/marketers-flunk-the-big-data-test.

7. Christopher S. Penn, "The Marketing Skills of the Future," Awaken Your Superhero, October 15, 2013, www.christopherspenn.com/2013/10/the-marketing-skills-of-the-future/.

8. Jeffrey K. Rohrs, *Audience: Marketing in the Age of Subscribers, Fans and Followers* (Hoboken, NJ: John Wiley & Sons, 2014).

9. "Email Marketing Benchmarks," MailChimp, accessed June 27, 2014, http://mailchimp.com/resources/research/email-marketing-benchmarks/.

10. "B2B Content Marketing: 2014 Benchmarks, Budgets, and Trends—North America," Content Marketing Institute and MarketingProfs, October 1, 2013, http://contentmarketinginstitute.com/2013/10/2014-b2b-content-marketing-research/.

11. "Mobile Path to Purchase: Five Key Findings," Google, November 2013, www.thinkwithgoogle.com/research-studies/mobile-path-to-purchase-5-key-findings.html.

12. "comScore Releases July 2013 U.S. Search Engine Rankings," comScore Inc., August 14, 2013, www.comscore.com/Insights/Press_Releases/2013/8/comScore_Releases_July_2013_US_Search_Engine_Rankings.

13. "Facts About Google and Competition," Google, accessed March 19, 2014, http://web.archive.org/web/20140305210448/http://www.google.com/competition/howgooglesearchworks.html.

14. "Seeing Between the Lines…of the Search and the Click," Kantar Media Compete, accessed March 19, 2014, http://success.compete.com/seeing-between-the-lines-of-the-search-and-the-click-whitepaper.

15. Rebecca Lieb and Jeremiah Owyang, "The Converged Media Imperative: How Brands Will Combine Paid, Owned and Earned Media," Altimeter Group, July 19, 2012, www.altimetergroup.com/research/reports/how-brands-must-combine-paid-owned-and-earned-media.

16. "Statistics," YouTube, accessed March 19, 2014, www.youtube.com/yt/press/statistics.html.

17. "Cisco Visual Networking Index: Forecast and Methodology, 2013–2018," Cisco, June 10, 2014, http://www.cisco.com/c/en/us/solutions/collateral/service-provider/ip-ngn-ip-next-generation-network/white_paper_c11-481360.html.

18. "The CMO's Guide to Marketing Org Structures," HubSpot, March 3, 2014, www.slideshare.net/HubSpot/the-cmos-guide-to-marketing-org-structure.

19. *The Digital Talent Gap: Developing Skills for Today's Digital Organizations*, Capgemini Consulting, 2012, http://ebooks.capgemini-consulting.com/The-Digital-Talent-Gap/index.html.

20. Abbey Lombardi, "Digital Marketing Skills Grow in Demand, Becoming Harder to Recruit," WANTED Technologies Corporation, October 30, 2013, www.wantedanalytics.com/insight/2013/10/30/digital-marketing-skills-grow-in-demand-becoming-harder-to-recruit/.

21. Heather R. Huhman, author and consultant, marketing talent interview by Tracy Lewis (Jan. 31, 2014 via email).

22. "The HubSpot Culture Code," HubSpot, March 20, 2013, www.slideshare.net/HubSpot/the-hubspot-culture-code-creating-a-company-we-love.

■ CHAPTER 4: CONSTRUCT AN INTERNAL MARKETING ACADEMY

1. "Marketing Rankings," *U.S. News & World Report*, accessed March 19, 2014, http://colleges.usnews.rankingsandreviews.com/best-colleges/rankings/business-marketing.

2. Rand Schulman, "Will Universities Evolve?," Content Marketing Institute, February 15, 2012, http://contentmarketinginstitute.com/2012/02/will-universities-evolve/.

3. Mark Schaefer, marketing author and business consultant, marketing education interview by Paul Roetzer (Jan. 28, 2014).

4. Jeffrey L. Cohen, author, speaking and distinguished lecturer; marketing education interview with Paul Roetzer (March 19, 2014).

5. Anant Agarwal, "Why Massive Open Online Courses (Still) Matter," TED Conferences, LLC, June 2013, www.ted.com/talks/anant_agarwal_why_massively_open_online_courses_still_matter.

6. George Siemens, "The Attack on Our Higher Education System—And Why We Should Welcome It," TED Conferences LLC, January 31, 2014, http://blog.ted.com/2014/01/31/the-attack-on-our-higher-education-system-and-why-we-should-welcome-it/.

7. "The State of Digital Marketing Talent," Online Marketing Institute, accessed March 19, 2014, http://learnit.onlinemarketinginstitute.org/

TalentGapReport.html?utm_source=blog&utm_medium=text&utm_camp aign=blog110513.

8. *The Digital Talent Gap: Developing Skills for Today's Digital Organizations*, Capgemini Consulting, 2012, http://ebooks.capgemini-consulting .com/The-Digital-Talent-Gap/index.html.

■ CHAPTER 5: PROPEL GROWTH THROUGH AGENCY PARTNERS

1. Paul Roetzer, *The Marketing Agency Blueprint: The Handbook for Building Hybrid PR, SEO, Content, Advertising, and Web Firms* (Hoboken, NJ: John Wiley & Sons, 2012).

2. Brian Whipple and Baiju Shah, "Turbulence for the CMO: Charting a Path for the Seamless Customer Experience," Accenture, April 22, 2013, www.accenture.com/us-en/Pages/insight-turbulence-cmo-summ ary.aspx.

3. "Ad Agencies Struggling to Evolve in Digital Age, Reports CMO Council; Clients Experience High Turnover of Interactive Marketing Firms," CMO Council, January 23, 2012, www.cmocouncil.org/cat_details.php?fid=219

4. "99designs," CrunchBase, accessed March 19, 2014, www.crunchbase .com/company/99designs.

5. "Contently," CrunchBase, accessed March 19, 2014, www.crunchbase .com/company/contently.

6. "crowdSPRING," CrunchBase, accessed March 19, 2014, www.crunchbase .com/company/crowdspring.

7. "DesignCrowd," CrunchBase, accessed March 19, 2014, www.crunchbase .com/company/designcrowd.

8. "Scripted," CrunchBase, accessed March 19, 2014, www.crunchbase .com/company/scripted.

9. "Textbroker," CrunchBase, accessed March 19, 2014, www.crunchbase .com/company/sario-marketing.

10. "Ad Agencies Struggling to Evolve in Digital Age, Reports CMO Council; Clients Experience High Turnover of Interactive Marketing Firms," CMO Council, January 23, 2012, http://www.cmocouncil.org/ press-detail.php?id=2943.

11. "The 2014 Marketing Score Report: An Inside Look at How Professionals Rate Their Marketing Potential and Performance," PR 20/20, December 10, 2013, http://www.themarketingscore.com/blog/bid/358790/ The-2014-Marketing-Score-Report-An-Inside-Look-at-How-Professionals-R ate-Their-Marketing-Potential-and-Performance.

■ CHAPTER 6: CREATE A CONNECTED CUSTOMER EXPERIENCE

1. "Dynamic Customer Journey," Altimeter Group, accessed March 19, 2014, www.altimetergroup.com/research/research-themes/dynamic-customer-journey.
2. Christopher Steiner, *Automate This: How Algorithms Took Over Our Markets, Our Jobs, and the World* (New York: Penguin Group, 2012).
3. Xavier Amatriain and Justin Basilico, "Netflix Recommendations: Beyond the 5 Stars (Part 1)," Netflix, April 6, 2012, http://techblog.netflix.com/2012/04/netflix-recommendations-beyond-5-stars.html.
4. Stacey Vanek Smith, "What's Behind the Future of Hit Movies? An Algorithm," Marketplace, July 19, 2013, www.marketplace.org/topics/business/whats-behind-future-hit-movies-algorithm.
5. David Zak, "Brown Down: UPS Drivers vs. the UPS Algorithm," *Fast Company*, January 3, 2013, www.fastcompany.com/3004319/brown-down-ups-drivers-vs-ups-algorithm.
6. Carl Benedikt Frey and Michael A. Osborne, "The Future of Employment: How Susceptible Are Jobs to Computerisation?," University of Oxford, September 17, 2013, www.oxfordmartin.ox.ac.uk/publications/view/1314.
7. "IBM Watson," IBM, accessed March 19, 2014, www-03.ibm.com/innovation/us/watson/.
8. Christopher Steiner, *Automate This: How Algorithms Took Over Our Markets, Our Jobs, and the World* (New York: Penguin Group, 2012), p. 119.
9. Megan Friedman, "Quotes: Ken Jennings on Watson's 'Jeopardy' Victory," *Time*, February 17, 2011, http://newsfeed.time.com/2011/02/17/quotes-ken-jennings-on-watsons-jeopardy-victory/.
10. Bruce Upbin, "IBM's Watson Gets Its First Piece of Business in Healthcare," *Forbes*, February 8, 2013, www.forbes.com/sites/bruceupbin/2013/02/08/ibms-watson-gets-its-first-piece-of-business-in-healthcare/.
11. "The New Multi-Screen World," Google, August 2012, www.thinkwithgoogle.com/research-studies/the-new-multi-screen-world-study.html.
12. Shane Walker, "Wearable Technology Report—2013," IHS Technology, October 31, 2013, https://technology.ihs.com/426704/wearable-technology-report-2013.
13. "Wearable Computing Devices, Like Apple's iWatch, Will Exceed 485 Million Annual Shipments by 2018," ABI Research, February 21, 2013, https://www.abiresearch.com/press/wearable-computing-devices-like-apples-iwatch-will.
14. Marcelo Ballve, "Wearable Gadgets Are Still Not Getting the Attention They Deserve—Here's Why They Will Create a Massive New Market,"

Business Insider, August 29, 2013, www.businessinsider.com/wearable-devices-create-a-new-market-2013-8.

15. "Tracking Cookie Information," All Things D, October 26, 2013, http://allthingsd.com/trackingcookies/#whatiscookie.

16. "Privacy and Tracking in a Post-Cookie World," Interactive Advertising Bureau, January 2014, www.iab.net/futureofcookie.

■ CHAPTER 7: MANAGE THE MARKETING TECHNOLOGY MATRIX

1. Marc Benioff, "Marc Benioff: How to Turn a Simple Idea into a High-Growth Company," Salesforce.com, March 8, 2013, http://blogs.salesforce.com/company/2013/03/how-to-turn-a-simple-idea-into-a-high-growth-company.html.

2. "About Us," Salesforce.com, accessed May 2, 2014, http://www.salesforce.com/company/.

3. "EXACTTARGET, INC. (ET) IPO," NASDAQ, accessed March 19, 2014, www.nasdaq.com/markets/ipos/company/exacttarget-inc-764866-68688.

4. "ELOQUA, INC. (ELOQ) IPO," NASDAQ, accessed March 19, 2014, www.nasdaq.com/markets/ipos/company/eloqua-inc-720646-68010.

5. "ExactTarget Acquires Pardot, Announces Vision to 'Redefine Marketing Automation,'" Salesforce.com, October 11, 2012, www.pardot.com/press/exacttarget-acquires-pardot-announces-vision-redefine-marketing-automation/.

6. "Public Market Investment Firms Invest $35 Million in HubSpot Mezzanine Round," HubSpot, November 5, 2012, www.hubspot.com/blog/bid/33794/Public-Market-Investment-Firms-Invest-35-Million-in-HubSpot-Mezzanine-Round.

7. "Oracle Buys Eloqua," Oracle, December 20, 2012, www.oracle.com/us/corporate/press/1887595.

8. "MARKETO, INC. (MKTO) IPO," NASDAQ, accessed March 19, 2014, www.nasdaq.com/markets/ipos/company/marketo-inc-827852-72170.

9. "Salesforce.com Signs Definitive Agreement to Acquire ExactTarget," Salesforce.com, June 4, 2013, www.salesforce.com/company/news-press/press-releases/2013/06/130604.jsp.

10. Scott Brinker, "Marketing Technology Landscape Infographic," Chief Marketing Technologist blog, August 3, 2011, http://chiefmartec.com/2011/08/marketing-technology-landscape-infographic/.

11. Scott Brinker, "Marketing Technology Landscape Supergraphic (2012)," Chief Marketing Technologist blog, September 5, 2012, http://chiefmartec.com/2012/09/marketing-technology-landscape-supergraphic-2012/.

12. Scott Brinker, "Marketing Technology Landscape Supergraphic (2014)," Chief Marketing Technologist blog, January 7, 2014, http://chiefmartec .com/2014/01/marketing-technology-landscape-supergraphic-2014/.

13. Scott Brinker, "Marketing Technology Landscape Supergraphic (2014)," Chief Marketing Technologist blog, January 7, 2014, http://chiefmartec .com/2014/01/marketing-technology-landscape-supergraphic-2014/.

14. "G2 Crowd," CrunchBase, accessed June 27, 2014, www.crunchbase .com/company/g2-crowd.

15. "TrustRadius," CrunchBase, accessed March 19, 2014, www.crunchbase .com/company/trustradius.

16. "Asana," CrunchBase, accessed March 19, 2014, www.crunchbase .com/company/asana.

17. "Basecamp," accessed May 2, 2014, https://basecamp.com/.

18. "Podio," accessed May 2, 2014, https://podio.com.

19. "HootSuite," CrunchBase, accessed June 27, 2014, www.crunchbase .com/company/hootsuite.

■ CHAPTER 8: PERFORM A MARKETING ASSESSMENT

1. "The 2014 Marketing Score Report: An Inside Look at How Professionals Rate Their Marketing Potential and Performance," PR 20/20, December 10, 2013, www.themarketingscore.com/blog/bid/358790/The-2014-Marketing-Score-Report-An-Inside-Look-at-How-Professionals-Rate-Their-Marketing-Potential-and-Performance.

2. Simon Sinek, "How Great Leaders Inspire Action," TED Conferences LLC, September 2009, www.ted.com/talks/simon_sinek_how_great_leaders_inspire_action.

■ CHAPTER 9: DEVELOP A MARKETING SCORECARD

1. "Digital Distress: What Keeps Marketers Up at Night?," Adobe Systems Incorporated, September 23, 2013, http://blogs.adobe.com/conversations/ 2013/09/digital-distress-what-keeps-marketers-up-at-night.html.

2. "Findings from the 2013 Joint Forrester, ITSMA, and VisionEdge Marketing Survey," ITSMA, May 21, 2013, www.itsma.com/news/findings-from-the-2013-joint-forrester-itsma-and-visionedge-marketing-survey/.

3. "About the Attribution Models," Google, accessed March 19, 2014, https:// support.google.com/analytics/answer/1665189.

■ CHAPTER 10: STRATEGIZE A MARKETING GAMEPLAN

1. "The 2014 Marketing Score Report: An Inside Look at How Professionals Rate Their Marketing Potential and Performance," PR 20/20, December 10, 2013, www.themarketingscore.com/blog/bid/358790/The-2014-Marketing-Score-Report-An-Inside-Look-at-How-Professionals-Rate-Their-Marketing-Potential-and-Performance.

About the Author

Paul Roetzer (@PaulRoetzer) is founder and CEO of PR 20/20 (@pr2020), an inbound marketing agency filled with modern marketers immersed in technology and obsessed with producing results. The agency's team runs integrated campaigns that build brand, generate leads, convert sales, and increase loyalty.

PR 20/20 was the first firm in HubSpot's certified Agency Partner program, which now includes more than 1,500 agencies worldwide. Roetzer's first book, *The Marketing Agency Blueprint* (John Wiley & Sons, 2012), serves as a guide for building tech-savvy, hybrid marketing agencies.

Roetzer frequently speaks at national and international events on the topics of agency management, content marketing, inbound marketing, marketing measurement and performance, public relations, social media, and strategy. He is the creator of Marketing Agency Insider (@agencyin), the hub for a more open and collaborative agency ecosystem, and Marketing Score (@MKTScore), a free online assessment tool and marketing intelligence engine. He also regularly contributes to the PR 20/20 blog at www.PR2020.com.

Index